Footprint Handbook
Bangalore
& Karnataka

DAVID S

This is
Karnataka

The chasm between rural Karnataka and its cosmopolitan capital Bengaluru can be shockingly wide. You enter via one of India's most exciting and urbane cities: switchboards hum with outsourced call centre traffic; world-class medics perform miracle heart and brain surgeries; and roads grind to a halt in rush-hour traffic. But within minutes of leaving the city behind, you enter a land that seems frozen in time: its red and black earth covered with tumbled mounds of granite boulders, its sugar cane still tugged to market by bullock cart, its villagers' concerns wholly agrarian.

Karnataka's interior has been seat to a roll-call of dynasties whose once-great cities now stand largely in dusty ruins. The exquisite Chalukyan and Hoysala temples of Pattadakal and Halebid meet their match in the Islamic palaces of Tipu Sultan in the south, and the onion-dome tombs of his Turkish and Persian antecedents in the northeast. The boulder-strewn ruins of Hampi are magic at any time of day; their glowing granitic desolation becomes utterly hypnotic at sunset.

In the forests of the Western Ghats you'll find some of India's richest wildlife habitat. Visit Nagarhole National Park in the dry season and you'll witness a Serengeti-esque spectacle, as elephants and deer gather in their hundreds to graze beside the Kabini River, taking their chances among the country's largest and best protected population of tiger and leopard.

Keep prodding within Karnataka's borders and you'll find a stretch of emerald-lush Arabian Sea coast that's every bit as idyllic as Goa's; one of the most powerful waterfalls in the world; and the town that invented South Indian vegetarian food.

Yet if this most dignified corner of India has a signature virtue, it is modesty. Karnataka hardly brags about its treasures. Which means that for now you can still enjoy them as an explorer, minus the crowds and package tourists.

David Stott

Best of
Karnataka

top things to do and see

❶ The Big Bull of Basavanagudi

Bengaluru doesn't wear history on its sleeve, but you can uncover traces of the capital's roots in Basavanagudi, a former farming village grown over in the city's madcap expansion. The 16th-century Bull Temple here houses one of the world's biggest idols of Nandi, Shiva's sacred bull, and is permanently thronged with devotees who flock to see the coal-black bull's daily anointment in butter. Page 13.

❷ Bengaluru's nightlife and shopping

From silk shops and unruly bazars to cosmopolitan cafés and India's coolest party scene, entertainment in Bengaluru is not in short supply. Wander the City Market by day, soaking up the noise and colour of the city's biggest flower market, then jostle your way into one of the hip bars or brewpubs along Church Street or Brigade Road. Pages 27 and 28.

❸ Mysore

The cultural capital of Karnataka, Mysore boasts an impressive royal heritage and a number of interesting palaces and temples, none more ostentatious than the Maharaja's Amba Vilas, illuminated on Sunday nights like a Christmas tree. Yogis flock to Mysore for its world-famous Ashtanga yoga centre, and the city's markets brim with sandalwood and silks. Page 34.

❹ Nagarhole National Park

One of India's top national parks, the serene forests of Nagarhole offer refuge to the country's largest and best-protected population of tiger and leopard, while elephant can be seen in their hundreds as they gather along the Kabini River backwaters in the dry season. A place of unspoilt wilderness, the park can be explored by jeep or boat. Page 46.

❺ Coorg

The lush green hills of Coorg are a popular weekend bolthole from Bengaluru, with a cool climate, beautiful scenery and any number of romantic hotels and homestays tucked away among the coffee plantations. One of the few areas to retain its ancient rosewood forests, Coorg offers gentle trekking and a distinctive local culture to explore. Page 50.

❻ Western Plateau – Belur, Halebid and Shravanabelagola

Karnataka's western plateau can be visited on a day trip from Bengaluru but merits a longer trip to fully appreciate the exquisite intricacies of the 12th-century Hoysala temples at Belur and Halebid, and the freestanding behemoth of Jain ascetic Bahubali – the world's tallest monolith. Page 56.

❼ Gokarna

Hippies and Hindus collide in this interesting pilgrimage town, with its stunning Om-shaped beach. The Shiva temple of Mahabaleshwara houses what is believed to be the original image of lord Shiva's lingam, while the clean stretches of sand are some of the most beautiful in India and still relatively undeveloped. Page 72.

❽ Hampi

Once the capital of the Vijayanagar empire, the sprawling ruins of Hampi are one of India's most important historical sites. Spread out across the banks of the Tungabhadra, amid sugarcane fields and rice paddies with a backdrop of intriguing rock formations, it's a powerfully surreal and hypnotic place that induces some visitors to stay for weeks. Page 80.

❾ Bijapur

Blessed with abundant mausoleums, mosques and palaces, dusty Bijapur feels like it's drifted in from the plains of North India, with a strong Islamic character that dates back to the dawn of the Deccani Sultanates in the 12th century. Dominated by the brooding tomb of Mohammed Adil Shah, whose looming hulk can be seen from 20 km away, the town is like an open-air museum. Page 89.

❿ Badami and Pattadakal

Badami, with its dramatic setting, and riverside Pattadakal are now quiet villages, but were once at the pinnacle of South Indian temple design. Dating from the sixth century, the beautiful rock-cut cave temples of Badami were once the capital of the mighty Chalukya empire, while those at Pattadakal have been recognized as a World Heritage Site. Pages 95 and 97.

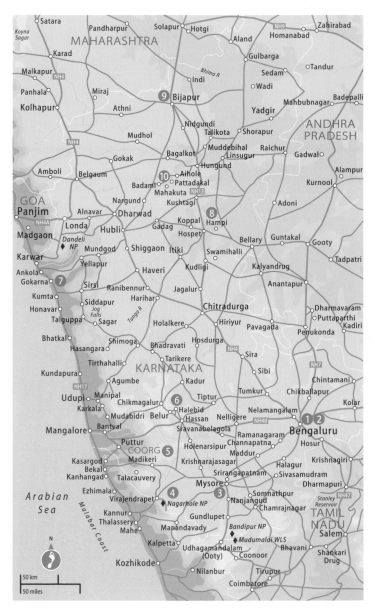

Commercial Street at dusk

Bengaluru
(Bangalore)

one of India's most progressive and cosmopolitan cities

IT capital Bengaluru, the subcontinent's fastest-growing city, is the poster boy of India's economic ascendance. Its buoyant economy is on display from the minute you hit the carpet-smooth six-lane motorway leading in from the swish new airport. In place of the elegant bungalows that once lined the streets of the British-built Cantonment area and the wealthy retirees who carefully tended their rose gardens are streets throttled with gridlocked traffic, a cosmopolitan café culture, a lively music scene and dynamic, liberal-minded people.

Yet for all its brewpubs, call centres and gleaming startup HQs, Bengaluru retains a grasp of its swirling, multi-layered past. The city has long been one of India's greatest producers of silk, and the clang and rattle of antique looms weaving gold-embroidered saris still rings forth from dingy workshops. In the crowded lanes near the City Market, around the great green lungs of Lal Bagh Gardens and Cubbon Park, fine buildings left over from the British preside over broad boulevards shaded by rain and flame trees. And if you walk around the jumbles of rope and silk shops, tailors, temples and mosques in the ramshackle and unruly bazars of Gandhi Nagar, Sivaji Nagar, Chickpet and City Market, you can almost forget the computer chip had ever been invented.

Essential Bengaluru (Bangalore)

Finding your feet

Bengaluru is very spread out and you need transport to get around. You also need to allow plenty of time: despite the new Metro and highway flyovers, infrastructure has completely failed to keep pace with the city's population explosion. Road travel at rush hours is best avoided, and even weekends can see the streets descend into something approaching gridlock. The Metro, touted as the city's salvation, is at the 'good start' stage: trains currently run along two short and as-yet unconnected stretches, one running east from MG Road, the other running north from Sampige Road (a few hundred metres north of Majestic) via Yesvantpur Station. Trains run 0600-2200. City buses run a frequent and inexpensive service throughout the city. Taxis and auto-rickshaws are available for trips around town, and should readily use their meters; they charge 50% extra after 2200. There are prepaid rickshaw booths at each of the stations. If you're planning on covering a lot of sights in a day it can work out cheaper to hire a car and driver – but bring a good book to while away the traffic jams.

Best places to eat
Karavalli, page 26
Daddy's Deli, page 26
MTR, page 25

When to go

By far the most comfortable time to visit Karnataka is October to March, when the weather is dry and relatively cool. April and May are intensely hot, with humidity building up as the monsoon approaches. The southwest monsoon arrives in early June, sweeping northward up the coast; the heaviest rain comes in July.

A second, lighter monsoon begins in September or October, travelling up the east coast and stretching inland to pour on Bengaluru. The post-monsoon period brings cool air and clear skies – this is the best time for mountain views – while winter temperatures can drop close to zero in the higher terrain of the Western Ghats.

Best places to stay

Sri Lakshmi Comforts, page 23
St Mark's Hotel, page 23
Taj West End, page 23
Vellara, page 23
Villa Pottipati, page 24

Weather Bengaluru

January	February	March	April	May	June
27°C 15°C 0mm	30°C 17°C 0mm	33°C 19°C 10mm	34°C 21°C 30mm	33°C 21°C 110mm	29°C 20°C 70mm

July	August	September	October	November	December
28°C 19°C 100mm	28°C 19°C 130mm	28°C 19°C 170mm	28°C 19°C 150mm	27°C 17°C 60mm	26°C 15°C 10mm

Time has not eroded the distinction in atmosphere between the 'native' city of Kempe Gowda and Tipu Sultan, contained within the crowded narrow lanes east of City Railway Station, and the broad elegant avenues of the Cantonment. In general you'll find the most atmospheric temples and historic sights in the former, while museums and monumental architecture congregate around the magnificent green lung of Cubbon Park further to the northeast.

Central and South Bengaluru

The centre of Kempe Gowda's city lies at the intersection of Avenue Road and Old Taluk Cutchery (OTC) Road, amid the bustling market area of **Chickpet**. It's worth braving the always-manic traffic to walk through the tangled knot of streets, where shops offering gold jewellery and silk saris jostle for space with peddlers of brass pots and 'fancy stores' selling *mehndi* cones and *bindis*.

City Market From Chickpet you can walk south to the City Market (officially known as **Krishnarajendra Market**, though most often called **KR Market**), for one of Bengaluru's most compelling visual spectacles. As the wholesale hub of Bengaluru's hyperactive flower industry, the basement of the four-storey building is a whirl of colour and noise from 0400 to 2230. There's a bewildering variety of specializations: you'll find growers coiling up long ropes of marigolds, porters manhandling coracle-sized baskets of jasmine blooms through the crowd, and open-sided stalls where workers convert those flowers into temple garlands and elaborate designs for weddings and film sets. The upper floors of the market are worth exploring, too, whether or not you're in the market for kitchen hardware or drill bits, and from the first floor there's a great view of the multicoloured scrum down below.

Summer Palace ⓘ *City Fort, 0800-1730, foreigners Rs 100, Indians Rs 10, video camera Rs 25.* West of the market lies the palace that Tipu Sultan, the perennial thorn in the side of the British, boasted was "the envy of heaven". Tipu's Summer Palace was begun by his father Haidar Ali and was completed by Tipu in 1789. Based on the Daria Daulat Bagh in Srirangapatnam, the understated two-storey structure is largely made of teak with walls and ceilings painted in brilliant colours with beautiful carvings. A room downstairs is given over to documenting Haidar and Tipu's reigns and their struggles against the British.

Lal Bagh ⓘ *Southeast of the Summer Palace, 0900-1830, Rs 10.* The botanical gardens of Lal Bagh were laid out across 97 ha by Haidar Ali in 1760 and are second only to Kolkata's in size. Tipu introduced a wealth of plants and trees from many countries (there are more than 1800 species of tropical, subtropical and medicinal plants) and the British added a bandstand and spectacular **glass house**, with echoes of London's Crystal Palace and Kew Gardens, home to flower shows in January and August. Sadly, the Indian affection for botanical beauty means

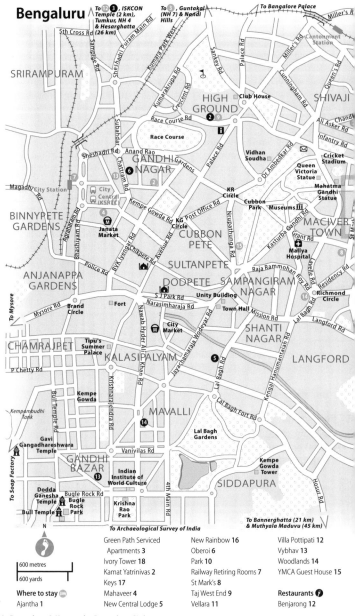

Bengaluru

To **3**, ISKCON Temple (2 km), Tumkur, NH 4 & Hesarghatta (26 km)

To **3**, Guntakal (NH 7) & Nandi Hills

To Bangalore Palace

Miller's R

5th Cross Rd

Cantonment Station

SRIRAMPURAM

Sheshadri Puram Main Rd

Kumara Park West

Samige Rd

SHIVAJI

Crescent Rd

Kumarakrupa Rd

Sankey Rd

Palace Rd

Queen's Rd

Miller's Rd

Cunningham Rd

HIGH GROUND
2 **9**
Club House

Race Course Rd

Ali Askar

Chand

Infantry Rd

Sheshadri Rd

Anand Rao

Race Course

Cricket Stadium

GANDHI NAGAR
6

Gardens

Palace Rd

Vidhan Soudha

Queen Victoria Statue

Magadhi

City Station

City Central (KSRTC)

Kempe Gowda Rd

KR Circle

Cubbon Park

Mahatma Gandhi Statue

Dr Ambedkar Rd

Kasturba Gandhi Rd

Museums

BINNYPETE GARDENS

4

Janata Market

Chikpete Rd

KG Post Office Rd

KG Circle

Avenue Rd

CUBBON PETE

Nrupathunga Rd

Grant Rd

MACIVER TOWN

St M

BVK Iyengar Rd

SULTANPETE

Mallya Hospital

Javelle Rd

Police Rd

Raja Rammohan Roy Rd

Residency Rd

ANJANAPPA GARDENS

DODPETE

SAMPANGIRAM NAGAR

Richmond Circle

14

To Mysore

Mysore Rd

Brand Circle

S T Park Rd

Unity Building

Narasimharaja Rd

Town Hall

Mission Rd

Langford Rd

CHAMRAJPET

Fort

Nawab Hyder Ali Khan Rd

City Market

SHANTI NAGAR

Lal Bagh Rd

LANGFORD

Tipu's Summer Palace

P Chetty Rd

KALASIPALYAM

Jayachamaraja Wodeyar Rd

5

Lal Bagh Rd

Kengal Hanumanaiah Rd

Kempe Gowda

Bull Temple Rd

Krishnarajendra Rd

MAVALLI

Lal Bagh Fort Rd

Kempambudhi Tank

14

Lal Bagh Gardens

Kempe Gowda Tower

Hosur Rd

Gavi Gangadhareshwara Temple

Vanivilas Rd

SIDDAPURA

GANDHI BAZAR

13

Indian Institute of World Culture

4th Main Rd

Dodda Ganesha Temple

Bugle Rock Rd

Bugle Rock Park

Krishna Rao Park

To Bannerghatta (21 km) & Muthyala Maduvu (45 km)

Bull Temple

N

To Soap Factory

To Archaeological Survey of India

600 metres

600 yards

Where to stay
Ajantha **1**

Green Path Serviced Apartments **3**
Ivory Tower **18**
Kamat Yatrinivas **2**
Keys **17**
Mahaveer **4**
New Central Lodge **5**

New Rainbow **16**
Oberoi **6**
Park **10**
Railway Retiring Rooms **7**
St Mark's **8**
Taj West End **9**
Vellara **11**

Villa Pottipati **12**
Vybhav **13**
Woodlands **14**
YMCA Guest House **15**

Restaurants
Benjarong **12**

M G Road area

that the rose gardens are kept behind bars. At dusk, Lal Bagh is popular with businessmen speed-walking off their paunches, and courting couples and newly-weds who sit on the banks of the lotus pond eating ice cream. The rocky knoll around the Kempe Gowda tower has great city views, and is popular at sunset. There are fortnightly Sunday evening performances of Kannada folk theatre, song and dance.

Around Lal Bagh Just off the northwest corner of Lal Bagh is the Dravida-style **Venkataramana Swamy Temple**, where the Wodeyar Maharaja chose to worship first after his dynasty's rule was reinstated at the end of the 18th century. The area is abuzz in the evening as hungry Bengalureans descend on the snack stalls and ice cream vendors of VV Puram's legendary 'food street'.

West of Lal Bagh, the hefty **Nandi bull at Bull Temple** ① *Bull Temple Rd, Basavanagudi, 0600-1300, 1600-2100*, was carved at the behest of Kempe Gowda, making it one of the city's oldest temples. The monolithic Nandi was believed to be growing unstoppably until a trident was slammed into his forehead: he now towers nearly 5 m high and is 6 m in length. His huge proportions, draped imperiously in jasmine garlands, are made of grey granite polished with a mixture of groundnut oil and charcoal. Under his hooves you can make out the *veena* or south Indian sitar on which he's resting. Behind him is a yoni-lingam. Just outside the temple are two bodhi trees, with serpent statues draped with sacred strands in offering for children.

To your right as you exit the temple lies **Bugle Rock Park**, a pretty little patch of wood whose trees are packed with

BACKGROUND

Bengaluru

Like any city worth its salt, Bengaluru comes complete with its own creation myth. Ballala, king of the Hoysalas, was on a hunt at dusk and became separated from his companions. Spying a lonely hut, he knocked on the door, and a woman took pity on the lost king, offering him a humble meal of beans. Ballala commemorated the kindness by naming the place *bbenda kalu ooru* (the place of boiled beans) and the name stuck.

Human habitation in the Bengaluru region stretches back to at least the Stone Age; megalithic tombs with iron tools dating to 1000 BC have been unearthed within the city limits, and Roman coins from the age of Augustus speak of a commercial centre boasting international connections at the dawn of the millennium.

The modern city of Bengaluru traces its origins to 1537, when the Yelahanka chieftain Kempe Gowda, a feudatory of the Vijayanagar Empire, built a mud fort and four watchtowers, visualizing them as the limits of a great future city. Muslim ruler Haidar Ali strengthened those fortifications, and built many splendid palaces and pleasure gardens, before his death at the hands of the British, leaving his son Tipu Sultan to pick up where he left off. During the Third Mysore War, in 1791, Tipu fought fiercely to hold the city against Earl Cornwallis, who marched down from Calcutta at the head of "the finest, best appointed [army] that ever took the field in India", but his most powerful fortress was taken by a stealthy attack following a siege in March 1791. Cornwallis took

fruit bats. It also holds one of Kempe Gowda's four 16th-century watchtowers. Also here is the **Dodda Ganesha Temple** ⓘ *open 0700-1230 and 1730-2030*, named for the towering idol of Ganesh – 18 feet high and 16 feet wide – also carved on the orders of Kempe Gowda.

Sri Gavi Gangadhareshwara Temple Northwest of here, the Sri Gavi Gangadhareshwara Temple dates back to the ninth-century Chola dynasty. Its most remarkable feature is the 'open window' to the left of the temple, which only once a year (on **Makara Sankrati Day**, 14/15 January) allows a shaft of light to shine between the horns of the stone Nandi bull in the courtyard and to then fall on the Siva lingam in the inner sanctum.

Palm Leaf Library ⓘ *No 33, 5th Main Rd, Chamarajpet*. For those interested in ancient Indian astrological practices, the Palm Leaf Library is supposed to be the repository for everyone's special leaf, which gives accurate details of character, past, present and future. Locating each leaf is not guaranteed.

control of a large town that was already established as an important manufacturing centre and, after Tipu's death in 1799, he installed the Wodeyar of Mysore as the ruler and the rajas developed Bengaluru into a major city. The Bangalore Cantonment was founded in 1806, and in 1831 the British shifted the capital from Mysore in favour of Bangalore's more congenial climate.

For the next century Bengaluru existed as two cities – the bustling Kannada-speaking 'native' City, and the multicultural Cantonment, dominated by the fixtures and fittings of the British military – parade grounds, genteel parks, churches, museums and cinemas – but also populated by immigrants from all over the country.

Bengaluru's great leap forward began in the wake of a devastating outbreak of bubonic plague in 1898, with the government investing in improved sanitation and health facilities in the city. Other innovations followed in a flood: in 1905 India's first electric light bulb fizzed to life in the City Market, and in 1911 the opening of the venerable Indian Institute of Science put the city on the map as a leader in education and research. Under successive Diwans of Mysore, notably M Vishvesvaraya and Sir Mirza Ismail, the city experienced a Golden Age, with high ideas guiding public architecture, urban design and education.

Shortly after Independence, J L Nehru identified Bengaluru as a potential "template of a modern India". The city has since emerged as a pioneering presence in fields ranging from medical science to space exploration, while the rise of home-grown IT companies such as Wipro and Infosys have helped cement the city as India's leading hub for the high-tech industries.

MG Road and around

Bestridden by the concrete spans of the new Metro, Mahatma Gandhi (MG) Road is one of Bengaluru's busiest commercial streets, lined with malls, bookshops, silk emporia, restaurants and hotels.

Cubbon Park At the western end of MG Road lies the 330-acre oasis of Cubbon Park, laid out in 1870 and named after Sir Mark Cubbon, the 19th-century Commissioner of Mysore State. This is one of India's most beautiful urban parks, and a wonderful place to wander at any time of day. Contained within the park's leafy confines are bandstands, fountains and temples, but also wild thickets of bamboo, granite outcrops and lakes where kites and kingfishers swoop for fish.

Standing out in bright red on the northern fringe of the park is the Greco-Colonial **Karnataka High Court**, which served as the seat of government until 1956 when it was replaced by the post-Independence granite of the **Vidhana Soudha**, the state's legislature and secretariat buildings, across the street.

Government Museum ⓘ *Kasturba Rd, T080-2286 4483, Tue-Sun 1000-1700, Rs 4.* This idiosyncratic and slightly dog-eared museum opened in 1886 and is one of the oldest museums in the country. There are 18 galleries. Downstairs teems with sculptures: a huge-breasted Durga and a 12th-century figure of Ganesh from Halebid sit alongside intricate relief carvings of Rama giving his ring to Hanuman, and there are Buddhas from as far afield as Bihar. An upstairs gallery holds beautiful miniatures in both Mysore and Deccan styles, including a painting of Krishnaraj Wodeyar looking wonderfully surly. There are also Neolithic finds from the Chandravalli excavations, and from the Indus Valley, especially Mohenjo Daro antiquities.

In the same complex, the **K Venkatappa Art Gallery** ① *Kasturba Rd, Cubbon Park, T080-2286 4483, Tue-Sun 1000-1700, Rs 4,* shows a small cross-section of work by the late painter (born 1887). His paintings of the southern hill stations give an insight into the Indian fetishization of all things pastoral, woody and above all cold. There is also the story and blueprints of his truncated design for the Amba Vilas Durbar Hall in Mysore and miniatures by revered painter Abanindranath Tajore (1871-1951), alongside a second portrait of Krishnaraj Wodeyar.

Visveswaraya Industrial and Technological Museum ① *Kasturba Rd, next to the Government Museum, Tue-Sun 1000-1800, Rs 15.* This museum will please engineering enthusiasts, especially the basement, which includes a 1917 steam wagon and India's oldest compact aircraft. Others might be left cold by exhibits on the 'hydrostatic paradox' or 'the invention of the hook and eye and zip fastener technology'. Upstairs is a wing devoted to educating the inhabitants of Bengaluru on genetic engineering. You might find the debate a little one-sided: "agricultural biotechnology is a process … for the benefit of mankind," it states in capital letters. A small corner (next to the placard thanking AstraZeneca, Novo Nordisk Education Foundation, Novozymes and Glaxo-SmithKline), is dubbed 'Concerns', but you can see how cloning and genetically strengthened 'golden' rice might seem more attractive when put in the context of the growling Indian belly.

Shivaji Nagar To the north of here is Shivaji Nagar, an interesting area to explore centred on the 19th-century **Russell Market** and **St Mary's Basilica**, established by French Catholics in 1799 following the defeat of Tipu Sultan. Bengaluru's oldest church, 'Arokya Marie' earned fame during the 1890s for her power to cure plague, and the basilica is still visited by people of all faiths in search of a miracle cure. For a few rupees you can buy a small stamped metal depiction of the part of your body that's suffering, drop it in the box, and await the results.

Ulsoor Lake East of here lies Ulsoor Lake, once a favourite swimming hole for British soldiers, now sadly polluted, and beyond, the trendy shopping and bar-hopping district of **Indira Nagar**.

North Bengaluru
Bangalore Palace ① *north of Cubbon Park, T080-2336 0818, 1000-1800, foreigners Rs 450, Indians Rs 200, camera Rs 450, video Rs 1000; frequent buses from Majestic/ Sivaji Nagar.* This grand, Tudor-style, built by Chamaraja Wodeyar in 1887, is an incongruous pastiche of Windsor Castle complete with battlements and Gothic

ON THE ROAD

Going back to Kannada

On November 1st 2014, Bangalore officially became the latest big Indian city to tread the path taken by Bombay, Madras and Calcutta, trading in the name thrust upon it by tone-deaf British colonists for a brave new life under a more authentic spelling of its indigenous name.

It is joined by 11 other Karnatakan cities and towns: Mysore (now Mysuru), Belgaum (Belagavi), Bellary (Ballari), Bijapur (Vijayapura), Chikamagalur (Chikkamagaluru), Gulbarga (Kalburgi), Hospet (Hosapete), Hubli (Hubballi), Mangalore (Mangaluru), Shimoga (Shivamoga) and Tumkur (Tumakuru).

The campaign to restore the distinctively Kannada 'u' to the end of Bengaluru has been underway for almost a decade, driven by Kannada language scholars and authors, most notably the Booker Prize-nominated UR Ananthamurthy, who died barely three months before his campaign came to fruition.

The plan to reclaim Kannada identity for the state's capital has been carried out with the dignity that seems to be Karnataka's signature civic virtue, free of the chauvinist chest-beating that Maharashtra's political elite deployed in jettisoning Bombay for Mumbai.

Yet the mass renaming isn't without its detractors. Bangalore – a name so synonymous with Indian technical and marketing genius that it became a verb (if you've ever lost your job to invisible lower-paid workers in a developing country, you've been Bangalored) – has serious brand equity, both globally and within the country's own English-speaking elite. Members of the city's highest corporate echelons took to Twitter to declaim against its Bengaluru-ization.

The widespread name changes also present a dilemma for any Karnataka guidebook: to embrace the new and sow confusion among readers, or to cling to the familiar like some nostalgic octogenarian colonist. After prolonged meditation and performing the appropriate Vedic rituals, we've decided to hitch our bullock cart to Bengaluru: the name change is too established to ignore. On the other hand, for Mysore-Mysuru et al, the new names are going to take years, even decades, to percolate into everyday usage. Hence, in this edition of the book we've decided to continue using the old names throughout the text, and include the new names in the heading for each section, or wherever most relevant.

arches. The entry ticket includes a tour of the Mysore mahahrajas' collection of art and family portraits.

Cantonment From the palace you can strike eastward to explore the residential section of the old Cantonment, where suburbs with names like Fraser Town and Cooke Town retain vestiges of old colonial romance. A handful of original bungalows are scattered throughout the area, with their imposing gates, curving driveways and pitched roofs, especially around Dixon Road in Cooke Town.

Indian tiger

The economic transformation of India has been one of the greatest business stories of modern times. Now acknowledged as major player in the fields of IT and pharmaceuticals, in the past five years the economy has been growing at close to 9% a year, largely thanks to an investment boom, and as stifling regulations have been lifted entrepreneurship has flourished.

So powerful has the economy become that, 67 years after independence, the colonized have turned colonizers. The global ambitions of 'India Inc' have become evident in a series of high-profile buyouts, none more symbolic than the Tata Corporation's US$13.2 billion acquisition of Anglo-Dutch steel giant Corus, a company whose ancestry can be traced to many of the companies that once symbolized Britain's industrial pre-eminence. Chairman Ratan Tata proudly boasted that the takeover was "the first step in showing that Indian industry can step outside its shores into an international market place as a global player". Tata has also snapped up such emblems of Englishness as Jaguar and Tetley Tea and, not content with taking over the world, has set itself to cultivating the ambitions of India's rapidly growing middle class. The Nano car, launched in 2009 with a price tag of less than US$1000, together with the Shubh Griha project in suburban Mumbai which sells new apartments for just US$10,000, has made the house-and-car lifestyle a realistic aspiration for millions of Indians.

How big a dent the global recession might put in India's plans for growth remains to be seen. The IT industry, dependent on outsourcing dollars from

Karnataka Chitrakala Parishath ① *Kumara Krupa Rd, www.karnatakachitrakala parishath.com, Mon-Sat 1000-1730, Rs 50, Indians Rs 10.* West of the palace is this privately owned art school and gallery with an understated but excellent collection of paintings and sculptures, displayed in 12 distinct galleries spanning styles from tribal to international modern art. There's a superb collection of Mysore religious paintings, detailed in gold and gesso, plus a handful of original paintings by Rauschenburg, two rooms dedicated to mystic Himalayan landscapes by Nicholas and Svetislav Roerich, and a strong collection of prints by N Krishna Reddy. The campus hosts frequent markets selling arts and crafts from all over India.

Malleswaram A few minutes further west, Malleswaram is a bastion of upper-class Bengaluru and has been home to many city notables including the painter Venkatappa. Most of the old bungalows have gone, but it's still worth a visit to see the **Shaivite Kadu Malleshwara Temple**, which predates the settlement by several hundred years and includes a *nagarkatte* (a platform where serpent stones are worshipped). Across the road is the recently unearthed **Nandishwara Temple**, saved from bulldozing thanks to a remarkable Nandi statue that spouts water from an underground channel on to a Shiva lingam.

the hard-hit US market, has suffered a profit slowdown and been forced to send workers on year-long sabbaticals. However, with most of the major banks being publicly owned, the country has been shielded from the worst excesses of the credit crunch, and the relatively low importance of exports – 22% of the economy, compared to China's 37% – puts India in a good position to survive comparatively unscathed.

A bigger issue for India is how to reduce poverty. Arundhati Roy, a notorious fly in the ointment of Indian triumphalism, wrote (in the days before Tata takeovers) that India, having nowhere else to colonize, has made its fortune by colonizing itself. Rich Indians, disconnected from the reality of where their money comes from, pay little regard to the plight of eight-year-old workers hammering fist-sized lumps of rock into powder in Karnataka's iron ore mines, or the villagers whose lands are repossessed so companies can build cars on the cheap. While the media trumpets the nation's new-found power to put men into space, Infosys executives into mansions and millions of rupees into cricketers' pockets, government reports suggest that 75% of people in India survive on less than Rs 20 per day. As much as 40% of the country still exists below the official poverty line, and statistics on child malnourishment (India has the third highest rate in the world, after Timor-L'Este and Yemen), infant mortality (2.1 million children die every year) and corruption (bribes worth Rs 9 billion a year are hoovered up from below-poverty-line households for basic public services such as policing and schooling) show that for all its progress, the economy still has an awful lot of growing up to do.

International Society for Krishna Consciousness Temple (ISKCON) temple complex ① *Hare Krishna Hill, 1R Block, Chord Rd, Rajaji Nagar, 0700-1300, 1615-2030.* This sprawling, modern temple complex holds five shrines, a multimedia cinema showing films on the Hare Krishna movement, lofty *gopurams* and the world's tallest *kalash shikara*. Around 9000 visitors make the pilgrimage every day; *bhajans* (religious songs) are sung daily.

Around Bengaluru

Whitefield Whitefield, 16 km east of Bengaluru, is the centre of the city's ongoing industrial revolution, and claims to be the fastest growing suburb in Asia. Once best known for the **Sai Baba Ashram** at Brindavan, if you venture out here now it's almost certain to be on business. Whitefield is home to innumerable industrial estates, IT parks and hospitals, not to mention the hotels, international schools and malls which service their employees.

Devanahalli At Devanahalli, 40 km north, stand the monumental walls of the fort where Tipu Sultan was born. Now partially in ruins, the 15th-century fort encircles a mellow village of temples and free-roaming sheep. From here a side road leads

Bengaluru: India's high-tech centre

The contemporary high-tech and biotech blossoming in Bengaluru (Bangalore) has deep roots: the city was consciously developed into India's research capital after Independence, with public sector units in electronics, aeronautical industry and telecoms established in the city, and educational institutions to match. National programmes of space research and aircraft design continue to be concentrated here, and it is home to the Indian Institute of Science.

towards the Nandi Hills, passing through interesting countryside strewn with temple-topped boulders, and vineyards with grapevines held aloft by great standing stones of hewn grey granite. **Grover** ⓘ *63 Raghunathapura, Devanahalli Rd, Doddaballapur, www.grovervineyards.inwww.grovervineyards.in*, is one of India's most highly regarded wineries. It offers a three-hour tour, tasting and lunch for Rs 850 on weekdays, Rs 1000 at weekends.

Nandidurg and the Nandi Hills Some 57 km north of Bengaluru lies Nandidurg, Tipu's fortified summer retreat in the Nandi Hills, set on top of a granite hill with sheer cliffs on three sides. 'The fort of Nandi', named after Siva's bull, was converted to a pocket-sized hill resort by the British. A drive around the short road encircling the forested hilltop offers great views in all directions, particularly from the 600-m-high cliff, known as 'Tipu's drop'. Within the fort walls is the fascinating **Yoganandeeshwara Temple**, built by the Cholas, whose dark interior is decorated from floor to ceiling with superb carvings.

At the foot of the hill, the ninth-century **Bhoganandeeswara Temple** (the two temples are related, and their locations are symbolic; Bhoga, referring to earthly enjoyment, is located on the plain, while its sister temple is set on high to symbolize the spiritual ascent toward yoga, or union with god) is a good example of the Nolamba style: its walls are quite plain but the stone windows feature carvings of Nataraja and Durga. The 16th century brought typical Vijayanagar period extensions such as the gopuram at the entrance. To get to Nandiburg, take a bus from the Central Bus Stand (ask for the Nandi Hill bus, not Nandidurga); they leave at 0730, 0830, 0930, returning at 1400, 1630, 1830.

Nrityagram ⓘ *30 km north of Bengaluru, T080-2846 6313, Tue-Sat 1000-1730.* Nrityagram is a dance village where young dancers learn all disciplines of traditional Indian dance. It was founded by the late Odissi dancer Protima Gauri. Guided tours include lunch, dance demonstrations and a short lecture.

Bannerghatta Bio Park ⓘ *22 km south of the city, T080-2782 8540, Wed-Mon 0900-1300, 1400-1700, Rs 200, Indians Rs 60 including safari; guide Rs 200, video camera Rs 150.* This park covers more than 100 sq km of dry deciduous forest, and is home to wild populations of elephant, bison, boar, deer and the occasional leopard. A

For decades, Western travel to India was synonymous with emaciated hippies, and backpackers' conversations invariably veered towards the scatological as everyone, at some stage, was sure to catch the dread 'Delhi belly'. It's a sign of the times that, although the British National Health Service failed to award India its whole back-up project in 2004, the country has become a very real alternative to private health care, representing huge cost reductions on surgery.

The centrepiece for this emerging industry is arguably Bengaluru, which has the largest number of systems of medicine approved by the World Health Organization in a single city: cardiac, neurology, cancer care and dentistry are just a few of the areas of specialization, and clients include the NHS and America's largest insurance company. Open-heart surgery will set you back US$4500 in Bengaluru, for example, as opposed to US$18,000 abroad. And afterwards, of course, you can recuperate at an Ayurveda resort. Lately Bengaluru has knitted its medical specialists with its IT cred to pioneer virtual medicine too, whereby cardiac experts in the city hold teleconferences with outposts up and down the subcontinent to treat emergencies, examine and monitor patients via phone, text and video, a method specialists at Narayana Hrudayalaya confidently predict will one day become the norm.

portion has been fenced and the Forest Department runs a range of minibus safaris to see tigers, bears and Asiatic lions at close range in almost-natural surroundings (many of the animals here have been rescued from circuses). The park also contains a butterfly garden and an unappealing zoo.

Channapatna and the Ramanagaram Hills Around 60 km west of the city on the Mysore highway, **Channapatna** is an unassuming town renowned for its handcrafted and highly colourful wooden toys, which are on sale at dozens of roadside shops. The town is surrounded by the extraordinary **Ramanagaram Hills**, which rear out of the surrounding plains in great domes of reddish granite. Popularly known as the 'Sholay Hills' for their starring role in the legendary 1975 Bollywood movie *Sholay*, these hilly outcrops and boulders also provided David Lean and Richard Goodwin the ideal filming location to capture the atmosphere of E M Forster's Barabar Cave for their film of *A Passage to India*; the lower cave sequences were filmed at Savandurga, 40 km north of Channapatna on the way to Magadi; ask at the **Lakshmi** store for directions or a guide. It's a stunning climb up **Kempi Gowda Hill**. There is also a small **forest park** and the upper caves at **Rama Dhavara**, 2 km from Ramanagaram. The caves are visible from the road and easy to find, though only false entrances were made for the film.

Tourist information

For events, pick up the fortnightly *Time Out* magazine (www.timeout bengaluru.net), and the bimonthly *City Info* (www.explocity.com). An excellent online resource is http://bangalore.burrp.com/events.

Karnataka State Tourism Development Corporation (KSTDC) *Head office, No 49, Khanija Bhavan, West Entrance, Race Course Rd, T080-2235 2901, www.kstdc.net. Mon-Sat 1000-1730, closed every 2nd Sat.* Booking counters for tours and hotels at Badami House, NR Sq, T080-4334 4334, also has counters at the airport and City Railway Station.

Karnataka Tourism House *8 Papanna Lane, St Mark's Rd, T080-4346 4351.* A one-stop shop for bookings and information.

India Tourism *KSFC Building, 48 Church St, T080-2558 5417. Mon-Fri 0930-1800, Sat 0900-1300.* Very helpful.

Where to stay

Cheap hotels share the streets of the ill-named Majestic district, northeast of the bus stand around SC (Subedar Chatram) Rd, with seedy bars and cinemas – a daunting prospect at night. MG Rd offers a more sanitized environment, and has rooms for every budget from backpacker to super-luxury. Top-end hotels can add 25% in taxes.

Central and South Bengaluru

$ Mahaveer *8/9 Tank Bund Rd, opposite the bus station, near City Railway Station, T080-3271 0384.* Basic and decaying place on a noisy road, but just about OK if you want to drop your bags after a long bus ride. The larger deluxe rooms at the back are quieter.

$ New Central Lodge *56 Infantry Rd, at the Central St end, T080-2559 2395.* 35 simple, rooms, clean enough, some with bath, hot water (0500-1000).

$ Railway Retiring Rooms *City Railway Station.* 23 rooms and cheaper dorm for passengers in transit.

$ Signature Inn *479 OTC Rd, Cottonpet, T080-4090 8204, www.thesignatureinn.in.* One of the better Majestic area cheapies, with well-maintained rooms and responsive staff. 24-hr checkout.

$ Vybhav *60 SC Rd down a passageway opposite Movieland Talkies, T080-2287 3997.* As basic as they come, and pretty grimy, but the rooms are relatively big and airy and some open onto a shared terrace where pot-bellied Brahmins hang out and chat. Good value.

MG Road and around

$$$$ Oberoi *39 MG Rd, T080-2558 5858, www.oberoihotels.com.* 160 superb rooms and suites with private sit-outs, all of which have views across the lush tropical gardens. Decent-sized swimming pool. Good restaurants, bar, spa and fitness centre, beauty salon.

$$$$ Taj West End
23 Race Course Rd, near railway, T080-6660 5660, www.tajhotels.com.
Charming 1887 colonial property set in beautiful gardens; much more than a business hotel. 117 immaculately appointed suites and rooms with balconies and verandas, Wi-Fi, flatscreen TV. There's also a splendidly restored Heritage Wing, dating from 1907. **Blue Ginger**, one of Bengaluru's most romantic garden restaurants, serves authentic Vietnamese food in low-lit jungly surroundings.

$$$$-$$$ St Mark's Hotel
4/1 St Mark's Rd, T080-4001 9000, www.stmarkshotel.com.
This friendly, intimate business hotel is one of the best high-end deals in the city. Smartly renovated rooms and excellent value suites come with free Wi-Fi, and there's an excellent restaurant plus a rooftop terrace offering great city views. A nearby spa sends therapists over to give free massages on Wed night. Price includes breakfast.

$$$ Ivory Tower
12th floor Barton Centre, 84 MG Rd, T080-4178 3333, www.hotelivorytower.com.
22 comfortable, spacious rooms with stunning views over the city. Huge beds, Wi-Fi, a/c, fridge, phone. Old fashioned but spotless, good value, friendly. Good terrace bar and restaurant onsite.

$$$-$ Woodlands Hotel
5 Raja Ram Mohan Roy Rd, Richmond Town, T080-2222 5111, info@woodlands.in.

Large but charming old-fashioned hotel with 240 rooms (some a/c) and cottages, with attached baths and fridge, good a/c restaurant, bar, coffee shop, exchange, safe, good location but calm, good value. Phone, satellite TV, lockers.

$$ Sri Lakshmi Comforts
117 MG Rd, in alley behind the LIC building, T080-2555 9388, www.slcomforts.com.
Excellent budget choice right amongst the MG Rd action, with spartan but clean rooms, friendly staff and a good thali restaurant.

$$-$ Ajantha
22A MG Rd, T080-2558 4321.
62 basic 'deluxe' rooms and much better value cottages with sitting areas and campbed-style beds, set in a calm compound filled with bougainvillea and pot plants. South Indian veg restaurant, helpful management.

$$-$ Vellara
126 Brigade Rd, T080-2536 9116, www.hotelvellara.com.
A grim exterior conceals one of the MG Rd area's best deals. 36 spacious and well-kept rooms, which get better the higher up you go. TV and phone in each room. The value and location are excellent. Recommended.

$ YMCA Guest House (City)
Nrupathunga Rd, near Cubbon Park, T080-2221 1848, www.ymcablr.net.
One of the best budget secrets in the city. The location is wonderfully peaceful, just across the fence from Cubbon Park, and many of the rooms open onto an indoor sports hall where you can sit like Caesar watching badminton or karate championships. Afternoon cricket matches, excellent café.

$ YHA Guest House and Programme Centre
Contact Mr Sridhara, KFC Building, 48 Church St, T080-2558 5417.

North and West Bengaluru

$$$$ ITC Windsor
Golf Course Rd, T080-2226 9898, www.itchotels.in.
Elegant and luxurious hotel based around a Raj-era manor house, with huge suites decked out in Edwardian finery and spacious rooms in the adjacent high-rise. The best rooms come with a private butler. Good pool and health club, but – unbelievably for a business hotel at this price – Wi-Fi costs extra.

$$$ Villa Pottipati
142 8th Cross, 4th Main Rd, Mallesaram, T080-2336 0777, www.neemranahotels.com.
Historic townhouse with 8 rooms, furnished with rosewood 4-poster neds and sepia Indian portrait photography. Set in a garden on the charming quiet tree-lined avenues of Bengaluru's Brahminical suburbs. A/c and internet facilities, small plunge pool. Atmospheric, but a bit lacklustre. Thin mattresses.

$$$-$$ Green Path Serviced Apartments
32/2 New BEL Rd, Seenappa Layout (north of centre near Hebbal flyover), T080-4266 4777, www.thegreenpath.in.
Comfortable and spacious if slightly anonymous 1- to 3-bedroom apartments. Built using renewable materials and run on eco principles including rainwater harvesting and solar-heated water. Facilities include Wi-Fi and bicycles to ride to the local shops. Price includes an organic breakfast.

Around Bengaluru

$$$$ Shreyas Bangalore
35 km northwest of town in Nelamangala, T080-2773 7102, www.shreyasretreat.com.
The place for peace and yoga in 5-star luxury, with twice-daily classes, silent meditations, Vedanta consultants and life coaching. Pampering includes Balinese massage and exotic fruit body scrubs, and the vegetarian cuisine is exceptional. Alcohol is forbidden, but there's a gym, book and DVD library, and in case you forgot you were in Bangalore, Wi-Fi throughout the property. 3- to 6-night packages start at around US$1500.

$$$$ Soukya International Holistic Health Centre
Whitefield, 17 km east of Bengaluru, T080-2810 7000, www.soukya.com.
This healing centre offers restorative, personalized programmes: detox, de-stress and weight loss, or relax with naturopathy and Ayurveda suited to asthma, diabetes, hypertension and addictions. Accommodation is in individual cottages around the lawns, surrounded by flowers and trees. Programmes cost US$200-500 a day.

$$$ Alila Bangalore
100/6, HAL-Varthur Main Rd, Whitefield, T080-7154 4444, www.alilahotels.com.
Attractive and efficient upscale hotel with 122 rooms and suites, all dressed for business with workstations and free Wi-Fi. The rooftop infinity pool, organic restaurant and chauffeur service make this a standout choice for the price in Whitefield.

$$$ Windflower Prakruthi
Hegganhalli Village, T080-4901 5777, www.thewindflower.com.

This appealing plant-filled resort set among mango orchards makes a good base for exploring the Nandi Hills and Devanahalli area. Spacious, well-equipped cottages come with huge sunken showers. Activities include ATV bikes, zorbing and a high-level ropes course. Packed at weekends, virtually empty midweek.

Restaurants

For excellent fresh, cheap, South Indian staples like *iddli*, *dosa* and *vada* look for branches of **Darshini**, **Shiv Sagar**, **Shanthi Sagar**, **Sukh Sagar** and **Kamat** all of which are hygienic and efficient restaurant chains. At the other end of the price scale, the Taj West End hotel has the Vietnamese restaurant **Blue Ginger**, while the Sunday all you-can-eat brunch at the **Leela** is popular with expats and the city's business elite. If you're missing international fast food head for **Brigade** and MG Rd and the food court at the **Forum** shopping mall. Chains of **Cafe Coffee Day** are ubiquitous.

Central and South Bengaluru

$ Food Street
VV Puram.
This small lane, leading south off Sajjan Rao Circle just west of Lal Bagh, is lined with food carts and cheap hole-in-the-wall snack stands. It's a hive of activity from 1900-2300. A roving repast here can have you sampling North Indian *chaats*, *idli*, *ragi roti*, Chinese fast food and Bengali sweets.

$ MTR (Mavalli Tiffin Rooms)
11 Lalbagh Rd, T080-222 0022. Tiffin 0600-1100 and 1530-1930, lunch 1230-1430 and 2000-2100. Closed Mon lunch.

Tip...
Look out for Grover wine, which is the product of the first French grape grown in Indian soil, sown 40 km from Bengaluru at the foot of the Nandi Hills. Veuve Clicquot has a stake in the company, which is now exporting to France.

The quintessential Bengaluru restaurant: a classic Kannadiga Brahmin vegetarian oozing 1920s atmosphere, full of Bengaluru elders, at the edge of Lalbagh gardens. A 14-course lunch lasts 2 hrs, but you'll be lucky to get a table. If you're in a hurry it does parcels to take away. The simple vegetarian food is superb, but people watching is half the fun.

$ Vidyarthi Bhavan
32 Gandhi Bazar, T080-2667 7588. Sat-Thu 0630-1130 and 1400-2000.
Unassuming vegetarian joint in the Basavanagudi district (near Nandi bull and Gandhi Bazar) whose Mysore masala dosa is justly famous, served with a side order of butter, coconut chutney and potato and onion curry. Open since 1938.

MG Road and around

$$$ Ebony Restaurant
Ivory Tower (see Where to stay), T080-6134 4880. Open 1230-1500 and 1930-2300.
Surprisingly good value lunch and dinner buffets (from Rs 395) at this penthouse terrace restaurant, which offers the best views in Bengaluru. Parsi dishes like mutton *dhansak* and curry *chawal*, along with Mughlai, Tandoori and French food. Good veg options.

$$$ Karavalli
*At the **Taj Gateway**, 166 Residency Rd, T080-6660 4519.*
The best high-end Indian restaurant in the city, offering upscale Karnataka coastal food.

$$ Benjarong
1/3 Ulsoor Rd, T080-3221 7201.
If you're craving Thai, this is the place. Expect charming service and authentic red curry, dished up with lots of extras.

$$ Coconut Grove
86 Spencer Building, Church St, T080-2559 6149.
Good varied Southern Indian menu, beers, buzzing place with sit-outs under shades.

$$ Daddy's Deli/Red Fork
594 12th Main Rd, off 100 Feet Rd, Indira Nagar, T4115 4372.
Warm and bright café in trendy Indira Nagar, serving first-class Parsi specials alongside brilliant salads and pasta dishes and proper coffee. Highly recommended.

$$ Ente Keralam
12/1 Ulsoor Rd, T3242 1002.
The best place in the city for high-end Keralite cooking – beef curries, fish thalis and tender coconut *payasam*.

$$ Koshy's
39 St Mark's Rd, T080-2221 3793. Open 0900-2330.
This humble, atmospheric restaurant-bar has been an absolute local favourite since the 1950s. Good grills and roasts, Syrian Christian fis curries and Sunday South Indian brunch. Also does Western breakfasts like baked beans on toast, cutlets, eggy bread or eggs any way you like. Stop at the kulfi stand on the kerb outside for a delicious, safe dessert.

$$ Tandoor
MG Rd, T080-2558 4620. Open 1230-1500 and 1900-2330.
Possibly the city's best North Indian restaurant, serving Punjabi, Muglai and Tandoori specialties.

$$ Truffles
22 St Marks Rd, T080-4965 2756.
The place to come if you're craving good Western fast food – proper burgers (beef and veggie versions), garlic mushrooms, sandwiches and cakes. Long queues at weekends, efficient home/hotel delivery service.

$ Chalukya
Race Course Rd, by the Taj West End Hotel.
Excellent vegetarian.

$ Natural Ice Cream
15/16 St Marks Rd.
One of several branches in the city, serving superb ice creams in exotic, totally natural flavours; the *chikku* and *sitaphal* (custard apple) are delicious.

$ Palmgrove
Ballal Residence Hotel, 74/3 III Cross, Residency Rd, T080-2559 7277.
Atmospheric place for Kannada Brahmin food, a/c, serves excellent giant lunch *thalis* for Rs 75.

$ Sweet Chariot Bakery
15/2 Residency Rd and branches all across the city. Open 1030-2030.
Excellent cakes and pastries.

North and West Bengaluru

$ Halli Mane
12 Sampige Rd, Malleswaram.
Fun and buzzing vegetarian canteen decked out like a village house: order at the counter, present your ticket at the relevant counter and elbow yourself a

bit of table space. A good place to try Karnataka specials like *ragi roti*.

Bars and clubs

Bengaluru is striving to reclaim its role as India's coolest party town: the pre-midnight curfew that once threw a wet blanket over the hard-rocking bars along Brigade Rd, Residency Rd and Church St has been pushed back to a more urbane 0100. Hotel bars are exempt from any curfew, and tend to offer a more refined atmosphere: those at the Taj West End have a particular Raj-esque elegance. Note that many of the better clubs have a hefty cover charge and a couples-only policy to prevent an oversupply of slavering stags.

13th Floor
Hotel Ivory Tower, 84 MG Rd, T080-4178 3355.
The least pretentious bar, with one of the best views of the city.

Church Street Social
46/1, Cobalt Building, Church St.
With a semi-industrial vibe and mismatched vintage furniture, this is a cool and friendly place for a quiet beer in the afternoon. On weekend nights the music reaches fever pitch.

Hard Rock Café
St Mark's Rd, T080-4124 2222.
Brand-phobics beware: this spanking-new venue is one of the hottest tickets in town, with a variety of drinking and dining spaces carved out of a lovely old library building.

Pecos
Rest House Rd, off Brigade Rd.
Connoisseurs of dinge should head directly here for cheap beer and hard-rockin' tunes.

Skyye Lounge
UB City, Vittal Mallya Rd, T080-4965 3219.
Stunning lounge and nightclub, with illuminated glass floor tiles and superb views from the open-air upper deck. The Rs 3000 cover charge ensures a smart but mixed crowd, dancing to hard house, lounge and R&B.

Toit
No 298, 100 Feet Rd, Indira Nagar, T0-1971 3388.
This multi-level brewpub-restaurant serves up excellent house-brewed beers, as accompaniment to good pizzas.

Entertainment

Bengaluru's heady cultural cut-and-thrust has put it at the Indian forefront of scenes from Carnatic classical music to heavy metal, and it's begun to attract big-name international touring artists. For an exhaustive but ill-edited list of what's going on around the city, check out www.allevents.in; or to find out about upcoming classical music concerts, http://kpjayan.wordpress.com.

Max Mueller Bhavan, *716 Chinmaya Mission Hospital Rd, Indira Nagar, T080-2520 5305, www.goethe.de.*
Film screenings, theatre and concerts.

Nadasurabhi, *www.nadasurabhi.org.*
Puts on monthly Carnatic classical concerts at a range of venues around the city.
Ranga Shankara, *36/2 8th Cross, II Phase, J P Nagar, www.rangashankara.org.* The city's most active theatre, with shows almost every evening (closed Mon) in English as well as in regional languages.
Ravindra Kalakshetra, *Jayachamaraja Rd, T080-2222 1271.* Kannada theatre and music.

Cultural centres

Alliance Française, *Millers Tank Bund Rd, off Thimmaiah Rd, opposite station, T080-4123 1340.*

British Library, *St Mark's Rd/Church St corner (Koshy's Bldg). Tue-Sat 1030-1830.*

Goethe Institut, *716 CMH RD, Indira Nagar, T080-2520 5305.*

Festivals

Jan/Aug **Lal Bagh Flower Show**, held on Republic Day (26 Jan) and Independence Day (15 Aug), with floral displays and sculptures.

Apr **Karaga**. Religious festival dedicated to the goddess Draupadi, in which men of the Thigala community, claimed to descend from the Veerakumars – a mythological army of the Mahabharata – walk on fire, beat themselves with swords, and compete for the honour of bearing an idol of the goddess on their head in a wild, drum-soaked procession through the old city.

Nov/Dec **Kadlekai Parishe** Centred around the Bull Temple, this 500-year-old harvest festival (literally 'groundnut fair') sees peanut farmers from all over South India offering their crops to Nandi. Sellers line the road with piles of raw, roasted and jiggery-coated peanuts in a riotous village-fair atmosphere.

Shopping

Bengaluru is a byword for shopping in India. **Commercial St**, **MG Rd** and **Brigade Rd** remain favourite hangouts for the city's youth.

Unless you want Western goods, though, the best shopping is to be had in and around the **City Market** (officially known as the KR Market) in Chickpet, where you can get silver, gold and silk saris; it's supposed to be the country's biggest silk wholesale/retail district and makes for some seriously fun people-watching when it comes alive at dusk. **Russell Market** in Shivajinagar is stuffed with vegetables, meat and antiques, while Gandhi Bazar in Basavanagudi is a fun place to stroll in the evening, with interesting clothes shops and excellent cheap food.

Shops and markets open early and close late (about 2000) but close 1300-1600.

Books

Blossom Book House, *84/6 Church St.* 4 storeys packed from floor to ceiling with new and second-hand titles.

Gangarams, *48 Church St.* Has a wide-ranging and expanding collection.

Sankar's, *15/2 Madras Bank Rd, T080-2558 6867.* One of the best in the city for new books.

Crafts and gifts

Karnataka is best known for silks, especially saris, and sandalwood products, from oils and incense to intricate carvings. Other local products include Mysore paintings (characterized by gold leaf and bright colours from vegetable and mineral dyes), *dhurries* (carpets incorporating floral and natural motifs, traditionally made from wool though cotton is now more widely used), inlaid woodwork and wooden toys and Channapatna dolls. Bidriware, a form of metalwork whereby silver and gold is inlaid or engraved onto copper and polished with zinc, originates from Bidar in the state's far northeast, but is produced throughout the state.

Watch out for private shops masquerading as branches of the government-owned 'Cottage Industries' chain. While the genuine article will have fixed, reasonably good prices, the (invariably slicker and more salesy) private operators will charge whatever the market will support.

Cauvery Crafts Emporium, *49 MG Rd.* Government-run shop specializing in Karnataka crafts, from cheap and colourful wooden toys to expensive sandalwood carvings.

Central Cottage Industries Emporium, *144 MG Rd.* Another government-owned shop, with fixed prices, carrying crafts from all over India.

Desi, *27 Patalamma St, near South End Circle.*

Kala Madhyam, *45 8th Main, 3rd Cross, Vasanth Nagar, T080-2234 0063, www. kalamadhyam.org.* NGO-run store showcasing artworks, metalwork, pottery, clothing and jewellery made by folk artists and tribal craftspeople throughout India. High quality.

Khadi Gramudyog, *Silver Jubilee Park Rd, near City Market.* For homespun cotton.

Mota Shopping Complex, *Brigade Rd.*

Orange Bicycle, *3353 5th Cross, 12th A Main, Indira Nagar.* Good for Indian kitschy gifts – T-shirts, bags, ornaments.

Raga, *A-13, Devatha Plaza, 131 Residency Rd.* Sells attractive gifts.

UP Handlooms, *8 Mahaveer Shopping Complex, Kempe Gowda Rd.*

Yellow Button Store, *787 12th Main, 1st Cross (Near Sony Center), Indira Nagar.* A careful selection of high-end homewares, decor and jewellery.

Jewellery

Most gold and jewellery is, logically enough, sold on Jewellers St in Shivaji Nagar, but also look along MG Rd, Brigade Rd, Residency Rd and Commercial St.

Silk and saris

Silk is, to many, what shopping in Bengaluru is really all about. There's a vast range available at the following shops.

Deepam, *MG Rd.* Fixed prices, excellent service, 24 hrs from placing an order to making up your designs.

Janardhana, *Unity Building, JC Rd.*

Maa Fabric Galleria, *36/1 Dickenson Rd, T080-4132 0384.* Small, hidden-away shop with a good selection of saris and high-quality silk by the metre. In the back room you can watch craftsmen block-printing designs, and with a few days' notice you can get them to make.

Silks Industries, *Jubilee Showroom, 44/45 Leo Complex, MG Rd.* Specializing in traditional Mysore Crepe designs.

Vijayalakshmi, *20/61 Blumoon Complex, Residency Rd.* Will also make shirts.

Golf

Bangalore Golf Club, *Sankey Rd, T080-2228 7980.* Foreign visitors pay US$30.

KGA Golf Club, *Golf Av, Kodihalli, Airport Rd, T080-4009 0000.* Rs 2000.

Horse racing

Bengaluru is famous for racing and stud farms.

Bangalore Turf Club, *Race Course Rd, T080-2226 2391, www.bangaloreraces. com.* Season May-Jul and Nov-Mar.

Swimming

The top hotels have become reluctant to let non-residents use their pools. However, there are good municipal pools, in varying states of maintenance, and some private clubs allow casual day visitors.

Builders NGV Club, *National Games Village, KHB, Koramangala, T080-2570 2247,* *www.buildersngvclub.com*. With swimming pool, badminton, billiards and tennis.

KC Reddy Swim Centre, *Sadhashi-vanagar near Sankey Tank*. 50-m pool and diving boards, open in 1-hr shifts from 0600-1000, 1230-15.30; ladies only 1530-1630.

Tour operators

Arjun Tours, *8 Bappanna Lane, St Marks Rd, T080-2221 7054, www.arjuntours.com*. Honest and reliable travel agency, good for car hire and hotel bookings, with safe English-speaking drivers. Recommended.

Bluefoot Culture Tours, *www.blue foot.in*. Kaveri Sinhji's personalized tours offer a behind-the-scenes look at life in Bengaluru. From in-depth explorations of classic city sights like the City Market, to breakfasts at obscure temples and encounters with local social entrepreneurs, the tours are professional and hugely informative. Highly recommended.

Clipper Holidays, *4 Magrath Rd, T080-2559 9032, www.clipperholidays.com*. Tours, treks (everything provided), Kerala backwaters, etc. Very helpful and efficient.

Golden Chariot, *Tourism House, Pappanna Lane, St Marks Rd, T080-4346 4342, www.goldenchariot.org*. A southern counterpart to Rajasthan's famous Palace on Wheels, offering luxurious train journeys through Karnataka, Kerala and Tamil Nadu.

Hammock Leisure Holidays, *Indira Nagar, T080-2521 9000, www. hammockholidays.com*. Tailor-made and small group trips around Karnataka and South India, including women-only group journeys.

Karnataka State Tourism Development Corporation (KSTDC), *runs tours from Badami House, opposite Corporation Office, T080-4334 4334, www.karnatakaholidays.net*.

Bangalore city sightseeing: half-day tours, covering Tipu's Palace, Bull Temple, Lal Bagh, Ulsoor Lake, Vidhan Soudha, Gava Gangadhareshwara Temple and the museums, runs 0730-1400 and 1400-1930; Rs 230, admissions extra, recommended. Full-day tour, to Rajarajeshwari Temple, HAL Museum, Bannerghatta Bio Park, ISKCON temple and more, 0715-2000, Rs 385-485, long and exhausting. Also runs Mysore and Srirangapatnam day tour, 0630-2330, Rs 650-850.

ITDC, *departing from Swiss Complex, No 33 Race Course Rd, T080-2238 6114*. Same schedule as KSTDC half-day tour but lasts from 0900-1700 and includes ISKCON, Rs 250. Mysore tour, daily, 0715-2300, Rs 600-700 including meals.

Trekking and adventure sports

Getoff Ur Ass, *858 1D Main Rd, T080-2672 2750, www.getoffurass.com*. The shop has camping and outdoor gear for sale and hire, while the owner organizes a variety of trekking and rafting trips in the Nilgiris and Western Ghats, plus kayaking and paragliding courses, photography workshops and camping weekends in private forest areas.

Walking tours

Bangalore Walks, *T(0)9845-523660, www. bangalorewalks.com*. Excellent guided tours of the city's cultural and historic landmarks, Rs 495 including brunch.

Transport

Air

Opened in 2008, **Bengaluru International Airport (BLR)**, T080-6678 2251, www.bengaluruairport.com, is the bold new face of Indian airports: it's gleaming, expensive, and the taxi touts in Arrivals greet you in suits. The domestic and international terminals are in the same building, around 35 km northeast of the city by a fast new road. Prepaid taxis in the terminal quote upwards of Rs 1500 to deliver you to the city centre, but perfectly comfortable and reliable metered a/c taxis queue outside Arrivals and work out at roughly half the price – around Rs 900 to MG Rd, or Rs 1100 to Whitefield. Airport buses run every 20-30 mins on 11 fixed routes to and from various parts of the city: Route BIAS-9 to Kempegowda Bus Station (Majestic) and Route BIAS-4 to Jeevan Bhima Nagar (via MG Rd) are the most useful for hotels. **KSRTC**, www.ksrtc. in, also runs twice-daily luxury coaches direct to Mysore at 1030 and 2100.

Bengaluru is becoming an increasingly important international hub, with direct flights to **London**, **Frankfurt** and **Paris**, as well as **Singapore**, **Kuala Lumpur** and many Gulf cities.

Daily domestic flights serve **Chennai**, **Coimbatore, Delhi, Goa, Guwahati, Hubli, Hyderabad, Jaipur, Kochi,**

Kolkata, **Mangalore**, **Mumbai**, **Pune** and **Thiruvananthapuram**. The best network is with **Air India (Indian Airlines)**, Unity Building, JC Rd, T080-2297 8427, airport T080-6678 5168, Reservations T141. **Indigo**, T080-2221 9810. **Jet Airways**, 1-4 M Block, Unity Bldg, JC Rd, T080-3989 3333. **Spicejet**, T080-2522 9792.

International Airline offices Air India, Unity Building, JC Rd, T080-2297 8447. **Air France** and **KLM/Northwest**, Sunrise Chambers, 22 Ulsoor Rd, T080-2555 9364, airport T080-6678 3109. **British Airways**, airport T080-6678 3160. **Cathay Pacific**, Taj West End, Race Course Rd, T080-4008 8400. **Emirates**, 3 Vittal Mallya Rd, T080-6629 4444. **Etihad**, Level 15 UB City, Vittal Mallya Rd, T1800-223901; **Gulf Air**, T080-2522 3106. **Interglobe Air Tansport (Air Mauritius, China Eastern, Delta, SAS, United Airlines**, 17-20 Richmond Towers, 12 Richmond Rd, T080-2224 4621. **Kuwait**, T080-2558 9841. **Lufthansa**, 44/42 Dickenson Rd, 080-2506 0800. **Nepal Airlines**, 205 Barton Center, MG Rd, T080-2559 7878. **Qatar Airways**, 307-310 Prestige Meridian, MG Rd, T080-4000 5333; **Singapore Airlines**, T080-2286 7870. **Sri Lankan**, Cears Plaza, Residency Rd, T080-4112 5207. **Thai Airways**, airport T080-4030 0396

Bus

City Bus Station (also formally known as **Kempegowda Bus Station**, and informally as simply '**Majestic**'), opposite the City Railway Station, is the very busy but well-organized departure point for services within the city.

Just to the south, the **Central Bus Station** handles long-distance buses run by the governments of **Karnataka**

(**KSRTC**), T080-2287 3377; **Andhra Pradesh (APSRTC)**, T080-2287 3915; **Kerala**, T080-2226 9508; and **Tamil Nadu (SETC)**, T080-2287 6975.

Computerized reservations are available on many services, from the booking counter. There are efficient, frequent and inexpensive services to all major cities in southern and central India. Frequent service to **Mysore** (3 hrs); several to **Hassan** (4 hrs), **Hyderabad**, **Madikeri** (6 hrs), **Madurai** (9 hrs), **Mangalore** (9 hrs), **Ooty** (7 hrs), **Puttaparthi** (4-5 hrs), **Tirupati** (6½ hrs). 'Deluxe' or 'ordinary' coaches run by private operators are usually more comfortable though a bit more expensive. They operate from opposite the Central Bus Station, and from outside Kalasipalyam Bus Station, 3 km to the south.

Car

Firms for city and out-of-town sightseeing include **Classic City Cabs**, T080-2238 6999; **Safe Wheels**, T080-2343 1333; **Angel City Cabs**, T091-6486 7774, driven by women and for female passengers only. Approximate rates are Rs 1000-2000 for 8 hrs or 80 km, then Rs 10-25 per extra kilometre, depending on the type of car. Rates for overnight or extended sightseeing will be higher, with additions for driver overnight charges and hill driving.

Taxi and autorickshaw

There are prepaid taxi booths at the airport and all 3 railway stations; prices should be clearly marked, and will be a little higher than the meter fare. Minimum charge in a meter taxi is Rs 125, which covers up to 5 km; Rs 10 per extra km. There are several reputable radio taxi companies with clean a/c vehicles and digital meters, including **EasyCabs**, T080-4343 4343, callcenter@ easycabs.com.

Autorickshaws should also operate on a meter system: Rs 25 for the first 2 km, Rs 13 per extra kilometre. In practice it can be hard to persuade drivers to use the meter, especially during rush hour.

Both taxi and rickshaw fares increase by half between 2300 and 0500.

Train
Bangalore City Railway Station
(formerly Bangalore Junction), opposite the City Bus Station, is the main departure point; enquiries T131, reservations T139. Computerized advance reservations are in the newer building on left of the entrance; No 14 is the 'Foreigners' Counter'. The Chief Reservations Officer is on the ground floor. Many trains also stop at **Cantonment Station**, T135, and an increasing number of important trains begin at **Yesvantpur Junction**, 10 km north of the city.

Unless stated departure times are from City Railway Station. **Arsikere** (for Belur and Halebid temples): *Siddhaganga Exp 12725*, 1300, 2½ hrs; **Chennai**: *Shatabdi Exp*, 1*2008*, daily except Tue, 1625, 5 hrs; *Lalbagh Exp 12608*, 0630, 5½ hrs; *Brindavan Exp 12640*, 1510, 5¼ hrs. **Goa** (Londa): *Ranichennamma Express 16589*, 2115, 11 hrs. **Hospet**: *Hampi Exp 16592*, 2200, 10 hrs. **Madurai**: *Tuticorin Exp 16236*, 2120, 10 hrs. **Hyderabad**: *Hazrat Nizamuddin Rajdhani Exp 22691/22693* 2020, 11½ hrs. **Thiruvananthapuram**: *Island Exp 16526*, 2140, 17 hrs, via Kochi (12½ hrs). **Mumbai (CST)**: *Udyan Exp 11302*, 2000, 24 hrs. **Maddur** and **Mysore**: *Chamundi Exp 16216*, 1815, 2½ hrs; *Tipu Express 12614*, 1500, 2½ hrs; *Shatabdi Exp 12007*, daily except Wed, 1100, 2 hrs.

Mysore &
Southern Maidan

The charming, unruly city of Mysore – the former capital of the princely state – does a brisk trade in shimmering silks, sandalwood and jasmine against a backdrop of the stunning, borderline gaudy, Indo-Saracenic palace. On the outskirts of the city is the empty ruin of Srirangapatnam, the island fortress of Britain's nemesis Tipu Sultan, and the bird-crammed Ranganathittu Sanctuary.

Further east is the Chennakesava Temple of Somnathpur, a spellbinding example of Hoysala architecture. Leopards and tigers stalk the two parklands, Bandipur and Nagarhole, that spill over Karnataka's borders into neighbouring Tamil Nadu and Kerala. Closer to the coast you can climb the Ghats to the tiny Kodagu district for forests of wild elephants and coffee plantations nursed by a warrior people. Also in Kodagu lies Sera, the university at the centre of one of India's biggest Tibetan Buddhist refugee settlements.

Mysore centre is a crowded jumble presided over by the gaudy, wondrous kitsch of the Maharaja's Palace, a profusion of turquoise-pink and layered with mirrors. But for some, Mysore's world renown is centred less on the palace, its silk production or sandalwood than on the yoga guru Sri Pattabhi Jois and his Mysore-style ashtanga yoga practice (see box, page 41). This all happens outside the chaotic centre, in the city's beautiful Brahmin suburbs, where wide boulevard-like streets are overhung with bougainvillea.

Sights

Maharaja's Palace ⓘ *Enter by south gate, T0821-243 4425, 1000-1730, Rs 200 includes audio guide, cameras must be left in lockers (free, you take the key), allow 2 hrs if you wish to see everything, guidebook Rs 10; go early to avoid the crowds; downstairs is fairly accessible for the disabled.* Also known as 'City Palace' (Amba Vilas), the Maharaja's Palace was designed by Henry Irwin and built in 1897 after a fire burnt down the old wooden incarnation. It is in the Indo-Saracenic style in grand proportions, with domes, arches and colonnades of carved pillars and shiny marble floors. The stained glass, wall paintings, ivory inlaid doors and the ornate golden throne (now displayed during Dasara) are remarkable. The fabulous collection of jewels is seldom displayed. Try to visit on a Sunday night, public holiday or festival when the palace is lit up with 50,000 fairy lights.

On the ground floor, visitors are led through the 'Car Passage' with cannons and carriages to the *Gombe thotti* (**Dolls' Pavilion**). This originally displayed dolls during **Dasara** and today houses a model of the old palace, European marble statues and the golden *howdah* (the maharaja used the battery-operated red and green bulbs on top of the canopy as stop and go signals to the *mahout*). The last is still used during **Dasara** but goddess Chamundeshwari rides on the elephant. The octagonal *Kalyana Mandap* (**Marriage Hall**), or Peacock Pavilion, south of the courtyard, has a beautiful stained-glass ceiling and excellent paintings of scenes from **Dasara** and other festivities

---

Essential Mysore and Southern Maidan

Finding your feet

Mysore is the transport hub for the region with long-distance bus and train connection with most major towns. The railway station is about 1 km to the northwest of the town centre while the three bus stands are all in the centre, within easy reach of the hotels. Despite being Karnataka's second biggest city, it is still comfortably compact enough to walk around, though there are plenty of autos and buses.

Best places to stay...

Green Hotel, Mysore, page 38
Orange County, Coorg, page 48
The Bison, Nagarhole, page 49

on 26 canvas panels. Note the exquisite details, especially of No 19. The **Portrait Gallery** and the **Period Furniture Room** lead off this pavilion.

On the first floor, a marble staircase leads to the magnificent **Durbar Hall**, a grand colonnaded hall measuring 47 m by 13 m with lavishly framed paintings by famous Indian artists. The asbestos-lined ceiling has paintings of Vishnu incarnations. A passage takes you past the beautifully ivory-on-wood inlaid door of the **Ganesh Temple**, to the **Amba Vilas** where private audiences (*Diwani-i-Khas*) were held. This exquisitely decorated hall has three doors. The central silver door depicts Vishnu's 10 incarnations and the eight *dikpalas* (directional guardians), with Krishna figures on the reverse (see the tiny Krishna on a leaf, kissing his toes), all done in *repoussé* on teak and rosewood. The room sports

Mysore

Where to stay 🛏
Bombay Tiffany's **1**
Green Hotel **10**
Greens' Boarding &
   Lodging **2**
Indus Valley **5**
Lalitha Mahal Palace **6**
Mayura Hoysala **11**
Mysore Dasaprakash **7**
Park Lane **9**

Ritz **4**
Royal Orchid Metropole **8**
Siddharta **3**

Restaurants 🍴
Amaravathi **1**
Anu's Bamboo
   Hut **2**
Jewel Rock **7**
Mylari **11**

Penguin Ice-cream
   Parlour **4**
Raghu Niwas **5**
RRR **6**
Samrat **12**
Shanghai **3**
Shilpashri **8**
Sri Rama Veg & Ashok
   Books **9**
SR Plantain Leaf **10**

ON THE ROAD

Medieval pageantry at Mysore

The brilliantly colourful festival of **Dasara** is celebrated with medieval pageantry for 10 days. Although the Dasara festival can be traced back to the Puranas and is widely observed across India, in the south it achieved its special prominence under the Vijayanagar kings. As the Mahanavami festival, it has been celebrated every year since it was sponsored by Raja Wodeyar in September 1610 at Srirangapatnam. It symbolizes the victory of goddess Chamundeswari (Durga) over the demon Mahishasura. On the last day a bedecked elephant with a golden *howdah* carrying the statue of the goddess processes from the palace through the city to Banni Mantap, about 5 km away, where the Banni tree is worshipped. The temple float festival takes place at a tank at the foot of Chamundi Hill and a car festival on top. In the evening there is a torchlight parade by the mounted guards who demonstrate their keen horsemanship and the night ends with a display of fireworks and all the public buildings are ablaze with fairy lights.

art nouveau style, possibly Belgian stained glass, cast iron pillars from Glasgow, carved wood ceiling, chandeliers, etched glass windows and the *pietra dura* on the floors.

The jewel-encrusted **Golden Throne** with its ornate steps, which some like to attribute to ancient Vedic times, was originally made of figwood decorated with ivory before it was padded out with gold, silver and jewels. Others trace its history to 1336 when the Vijayanagar kings 'found' it before passing it on to the Wodeyars who continue to use it during **Dasara**.

Maharaja's Residence ⓘ *1000-1730, Rs 20, no photography*. This is now a slightly underwhelming museum. The ground floor, with a courtyard, displays children's toys, musical instruments, costumes and several portraits. The upper floor has a small weapon collection.

Jayachamarajendra Art Gallery ⓘ *A block west of the palace, 0800-1700, Rs 25, no photography*. Housed in the smaller Jagan Mohan Palace (1861), the gallery holds a priceless collection of artworks from Mysore's erstwhile rulers, including Indian miniature paintings and works by Raja Ravi Varma and Nicholas Roerich. There's also an exhibition of ceramics, stone, ivory, sandalwood, antique furniture and old musical instruments. Sadly, there are no descriptions or guidebooks and many items are randomly displayed.

Devaraja Market North of KR Circle, this is one of India's most atmospheric markets: visit at noon when it's injected with fresh pickings of marigolds and jasmines. The bigger flowers are stitched onto a thread and wrapped into rolls which arrived heaped in hessian sacks stacked on the heads of farmers.

Chamundi Hill ⓘ *Immediately to the southeast of town, temple 0600-1400, 1530-1800, 1915-2100; vehicle toll Rs 30, City Bus No 185.* On the hill is a temple to Durga (Chamundeswari), guardian deity to the Wodeyars, celebrating her victory over the buffalo god. There are lovely views, and a giant Nandi, carved in 1659, on the road down. Walk to it along the trail from the top and be picked up by a car later or catch a return bus from the road. If you continue along the trail you will end up having to get a rickshaw back, instead of a bus.

Sandalwood Oil Factory ⓘ *T0821-248 3651, Mon-Sat 0900-1100, 1400-1600 (prior permission required), no photography inside. This is* where the oil is extracted and incense is made. The shop sells soap, incense sticks and other sandalwood items.

Silk Factory ⓘ *Manathavadi Rd, T0821-248 1803, Mon-Sat 0930-1630, no photography.* Here weavers produce Mysore silk saris, often with gold *zari* work. Staff will show you the process from thread winding to jacquard weaving, but they speak little English. The shop sells saris from Rs 3000. Good walks are possible in the Government House if the guard at the gate allows you in.

Sri Mahalingeshwara Temple ⓘ *12 km from Mysore, 1 km off the Bhogadi road (right turn after K Hemmanahalli, beyond Mysore University Campus), taxi or auto-rickshaw.* This 800-year-old Hoysala Temple has been carefully restored by local villagers under the supervision of the Archaeological Survey of India. The structure is an authentic replica of the old temple: here, too, the low ceiling encourages humility by forcing the worshipper to bow before the shrine. The surrounding garden has been planted with herbs and saplings, including some rare medicinal trees, and provides a tranquil spot away from the city.

Listings Mysore *map p35*

Tourist information

Department of Tourism
Old Exhibition Building, Irwin Rd, T0821-242 2096, www.mysore.nic.in. Open 1000-1730. See also www. karnataka.com/tourism/mysore. There are information counters at the train station and bus stand.

Karnataka State Tourism Development Corporation (KSTDC) *Yatri Nivas, 2 JLB Rd, T0821-242 3652.* Efficient.

Where to stay

May is the most important wedding month and so hotels get booked in advance. In the expensive hotels sales tax on food, luxury tax on rooms and a service charge can increase the bill significantly. The Gandhi Square area has some Indian-style hotels which are clean and good value. Note that JLB Rd is Jhansi Lakshmi Bai Rd, B-N Rd is Bengaluru-Nilgiri Rd.

$$$$-$$$ Lalitha Mahal Palace (ITDC) *Narasipur Rd, Siddartha Nagar T0821-252 6100, www.lalithamahalpalace.in.*

54 rooms and suites in the palace built in 1931 for the maharaja's non-vegetarian, foreign guests. In a regal setting near Chamundi Hill, it's an old-fashioned place with some original baths and an extraordinary spraying system. For nostalgia stay in the old wing. There's an attractive pool, but avoid the below par restaurant.

$$$$-$$$ Royal Orchid Metropole
5 JLB Rd, T0821-425 5566,
www.royalorchidhotels.com.
After languishing in disrepair for years, the Karnataka government has resuscitated the glorious colonial **Metropole** building. Airy rooms with high ceilings, massage and yoga classes, plus a small pool and excellent restaurant.

$$$$-$$ Green Hotel
Chittaranjan Palace, 2270 Vinoba Rd, Jayalakshmipuram (near Mysore University), T0821-251 2536, www.green hotelindia.com.
The princess's beautiful palace has been lovingly converted with strong sustainable tourism ethos: hot water from solar panels, profits to charity and staff recruited from less advantaged groups. The best of the 31 rooms are in the palace but if you stay in the cheaper, newer block you can still loll about in the huge upper lounges and enjoy the excellent library, chess tables and day beds. Unique, but beyond walking distance from Mysore centre.

$$$-$$ Indus Valley
Near Lalitha Mahal (see above), T0821-247 3437, www.ayurindus.com.
Family-run health resort in a splendid location, halfway up a hill. There are 22 rooms (in the main building or in a cottage), hot showers and Western toilets, TV in lounge, Ayurvedic massage, pleasant walks, vegetarian Ayurvedic restaurant, herbal wines and friendly staff.

$$$-$ Mayura Hoysala (KSTDC)
2 JLB Rd, T0821-242 6160.
20 rooms in this lovely, ochre-painted, ramshackle Raj-style hotel: it's full of chintzy soft furnishings, overspilling with plant pots; en suite bathrooms have both Western and squat loos; tiny whitewashed cane stools are propped up on terracing along with mismatched 1970s furniture. Facilities include 3 restaurants, a bar and a tourist desk.

$$$-$ Siddharta
73/1 Guest House Rd, Nazarabad, T0821-428 0999, www.hotelsiddharta.com.
105 rooms, some a/c, huge with baths, good restaurant (Indian vegetarian), exchange, immaculate, well run.

$$-$ Bombay Tiffany's
313 Sayyaji Rao Rd, T0821-243 5255, bombaytiffanys@yahoo.com.
60 clean rooms (12 a/c in the new hotel). The regular rooms are spartan, but the deluxe and a/c ones are very good value. Affable owner.

$$-$ Mysore Dasaprakash
Gandhi Sq, T0821-244 2444, www.mysoredasaprakashgroup.com.
144 rooms in this labyrinthine blue-white complex set arround an attractive, large courtyard. Milk coffee-coloured rooms are stocked with wood furniture and scrupulously clean white sheets. Peaceful and quiet despite being slap bang in the centre.

$ Greens' Boarding and Lodging
2722/2 Curzon Park Rd, T0821-242 2415.
Dark hallways give way to green gloss-painted rooms with dark wood furniture. Cool, spacious, central and darn cheap, but bathrooms are not the best.

$ Hotel Ritz
Bengaluru–Nilgiri Rd near Central Bus Station, T0821-242 2668, www.hotelritzmysore.com.
Bags of character in this 60-year-old house and garden set back from the busy road. 4 rooms with wooden furniture off cool communal area with TV, dining table and chairs. Pleasant open shaded courtyard. Legendary amongst backpackers so book ahead.

$ Park Lane
2720 Sri Harsha Rd, T0821-400 3500, www.parklanemysore.com.
Freshly renovated, with a price hike to match, but the folk-art-rustic rooms are clean and still good value. The noise, including nightly classical Indian performances, from popular downstairs restaurant does travel (open 1030-2330).

Restaurants

$$$ Green Hotel
See Where to stay.
Atmospheric with food served in the palace itself, on a veranda, or under the stars in the hotel's immaculate garden. But not the best food.

$$ Park Lane
See Where to stay.
Red lights hang from the creeper-covered trellis over this courtyard restaurant: turn them on for service. Superb classical music played every evening 1900-2130. Good food, including barbecue nights. Popular, lively and idiosyncratic.

$$ Shanghai
Vinoba Rd. Open 1100-1500, 1830-2300.
Superb Chinese food, despite the shabby interior.

$$ Shilpashri
Gandhi Sq.
Comfortable rooftop restaurant serving reasonably priced tourist-orientated dishes and chilled beers. Friendly but service can be slow.

$ Amaravathi (Roopa's)
Hardinge Circle.
Excellent, spicy hot Andhra meals served on banana leaves.

$ Anu's Bamboo Hut
367 2nd Main, 3rd Stage, Gokulam, T0821-428 9492.
Friendly little rooftop café in the midst of the Western yogi ghetto of Gokulam. The vegetarian buffet (daily except Thu, 1300-1500) is packed with salads and bean dishes, and always sells out quickly; Anu also does good smoothies and lassies from 1700-1900, and offers vegetarian cooking classes. Call ahead.

$ Jewel Rock
Maurya Residency, Sri Harsha Rd.
Dark interior, great chicken tikka, spicy cashew nut chicken, go early to avoid the queues.

$ Mylari
Hotel Mahadeshwara, Nazarbad Main Rd (ask a rickshaw driver). Open in the mornings until 1100.
The best *dosas* in town served on a banana leaf. The surroundings are basic and you may have to queue. The biriyanis are also legendary.

$ Mysore Dasaprakash
See Where to stay.
Good breakfast, huge southern *thali* (Rs 25).

$ Om Shanti
Siddharta (see Where to stay).
Pure vegetarian thali place, with a/c and non-a/c sections, thronged

with domestic tourists which is a fair reflection of its culinary prowess.

$ RRR
Gandhi Sq.
Part a/c, tasty non-vegetarian food served on plantain leaves, good for lunch.

$ Samrat
Next to Indra Bhavan, Dhanvantri Rd.
Offers a range of tasty North Indian vegetarian dishes.

$ SR Plantain Leaf (Chalukya's)
Rajkamal Talkies Rd.
Decent vegetarian *thalis* served on a banana leaf; also does tandoori chicken.

Cafés and snacks

Bombay Tiffany's
Devraja Market Building.
Try the 'Mysore pak', a ghee-laden sweet.

Indra Café
Sayaji Rd, on the fringes of the market.
Excellent *bhel puri*, *sev puri* and *channa puri*.

Penguin Ice-cream Parlour
Near KR Hospital, Dhanavantri Rd.
Sofas shared with local teens listening to Hindi pop.

Raghu Niwas
B-N Rd, opposite Ritz.
Does very good breakfasts.

Sri Rama Veg
397 Dhanvantri Rd.
Serves fast food and good juices.

The best bars are in hotels (see Where to stay): try the expensive but elegant **Lalitha Mahal Palace** or the funky lounge at the **Adhi Manor**, Chandragupta Rd.

Mar-Apr **Temple car festival** with a 15-day fair, at the picturesque town of Nanjangud, 23 km south (Erode road); **Vairamudi** festival which lasts 6 days when deities are adorned with 3 diamond crowns, at Melkote Temple, 52 km.
11 Aug **Feast of St Philomena**, 0800-1800, the statue of the saint is taken out in procession through the city streets ending with a service at the Gothic, stained-glass-laden cathedral.
End Sep to early-Oct **Dasara**, see box, page 36.

Books
Ashok, *Dhanvantri Rd, T0821-243 5533.* Excellent selection.

Clothing
For silks at good prices, try Sayaji Rao Rd but beware those pretending to be government emporia.
Badshah's, *20 Devraj Urs Rd, T0821-242 9799.* Beautifully finished *salwar kameez.* Mr Yasin speaks good English.
Craft Emporium, *middle part of Vinoba Rd.* Good selection and quality. Also sells cloth.
Karnataka Silk Industry, *Mananthody Rd, T0821-248 1803. Mon-Sat 1030-1200, 1500-1630.* Watch machine weaving at the factory shop.

Handicrafts
Superb carved figures, sandalwood and rosewood items, silks, incense sticks, handicrafts. The main shopping area is Sayaji Rao Rd.
Cauvery Arts & Crafts Emporium, *Sayyaji Rao Rd.* For sandalwood and rosewood items, closed Thu (non-receipt of parcel reported by traveller).

ON THE ROAD
Power yoga

If you know the primary series, speak fluent *ujayyi* breath and know about the *mulla bandha* odds are that you have heard the name of Sri Pattabhi Jois, too. His is the version of yoga that has most percolated contemporary Western practice (it's competitive enough for the type-A modern societies we live in, some argue), and although for most of the years of his teaching he had just a handful of students, things have certainly changed.

Though the Guru left his body in May 2009, a steady flow of international students still make the pilgrimage to his Ashtanga Yoga Nilayam in Mysore, where his daughter Saraswathi and grandson Sharath Rangaswamy continue the lineage.

Saraswathi's classes are deemed suitable for Ashtanga novices, but studying with Sharath is not for dilettante yogis; the Westerners here are extremely ardent about their practice – mostly teachers themselves – and there is a strict pecking order which first-timers could find alienating. Classes start from first light at 0400, and the day's teaching is over by 0700, leaving you free for the rest of the day.

There's no rule that says you must know the series, but it might be better, and cheaper, to dip a toe in somewhere a bit less hardcore and far-flung, such as Purple Valley in Goa.

For details and Sharath's teaching schedule, see www.kpjayi.com.

Devaraja Market, *North of KR Circle*. Lanes of stalls selling spices, perfumes and much more; including a good 'antique' shop (fixed price) with excellent sandalwood and rosewood items. Worth visiting.
Ganesh, *532 Dhanvantri Rd*.
Shankar, *12 Dhanvantri Rd*.
Sri Lakshmi Fine Arts & Crafts, *opposite the zoo; also has a factory shop at 2226 Sawday Rd, Mandi Mohalla*.

What to do

Body and soul
Jois Ashtanga Yoga Research Institute, *www.kpjayi.org*. Not for dilettante yogis at Rs 8000 a month, the minimum period offered.
Sri Patanjali Yogashala, *Parakala Mutt, next to Jaganmohan Palace*. Ashtanga

Vinyasa yoga; daily instruction in English from BNS Iyengar, 0600-0900, 1600-1900, US$100 per month: some say the conditions here are slapdash, although teaching is good.

Swimming
Mysore University, *2 km east of the palace in Saraswathipuram*. Olympic-sized pool, hourly sessions 0630-0830 then 1500-1600, women only 1600-1700.
Southern Star Mysore, *13-14 Vinoba Rd, T0821-242 1689, www.ushalexushotels.com*. More of a pool to relax by and sunbathe.

Tour operators
KSTDC, *Yatri Nivas hotel, 2 JLB Rd, T0821-242 3492*. **Mysore**, daily 0715-2030, Rs 155, tours of local sights and Chamundi Hill, Kukkara Halli Lake, Somanathapura,

Srirangapatnam and Brindavan Gardens. Tours also run to **Belur**, **Halebid**, and **Sravanabelagola** if there are 10 or more guests: a long and tiring day, but worth it if you are not travelling to Hassan. Seagull Travels, *8 Hotel Ramanashree Complex, BN Rd, T0821-426 0054*. Good for cars, drivers, flights, wildlife tours, etc, helpful. Skyway International Travels, *No 370/4, Jansi Laxmibai Rd, T0821-244 4444, www.skywaytour.com*. Excellent travel agency for car hire and accommodation bookings. TCI, *Gandhi Sq, T0821-526 0294*. Very pleasant and helpful.

Transport

Bus
Local City bus station, southeast of KR Circle, T0821-242 5819. To **Silk Weaving Centre**, Nos 1, 2, 4 and 8; **Brindavan Gardens**, No 303; **Chamundi Hill**, No 201; **Srirangapatnam**, No 313. **Central Bus Station**, T0821-2529853. **Bandipur**, Platform 9, **Ooty** etc, Platform 11.

Long distance There are 2 bus stations. **Central**, T0821-252 0853, is mainly used by long-distance **SRTC** companies of Karnataka, Tamil Nadu and Kerala, all of which run regular daily services between Mysore and other major cities. The bus station has a list of buses with reserved places. To **Bengaluru**: every 15 mins from non-stop platform. Also frequent services to **Hassan**, 3 hrs; **Mangalore** (7 hrs); and **Ooty** (5 hrs) via **Bandipur** (2 hrs). Daily services to **Coimbatore**; **Gokarna** (12 hrs); **Hospet**: 1930 (10 hrs), very tiring; **Kochi**, 10 hrs; **Kozhikode** via **Wayanad**; **Salem** (7 hrs); **Thiruvananthapuram** (Super deluxe,

14 hrs). Several to **Satyamangalam** (3-4 hrs) where you can connect with buses to Tamil Nadu. The journey is through wilderness and forests with spectacular scenery as the road finally plunges from the plateau down to the plains.

The **Suburban** and **Private bus stands**, T0821-244 3490, serve nearby destinations including **Somnathpur**, around 1 hr direct, or longer via Bannur or via Narasipur. Many private companies near Gandhi Sq operate overnight sleepers and interstate buses which may be faster and marginally less uncomfortable. Book ahead for busy routes.

Car
Travel companies and **KSTDC** charge about Rs 700 (4 hrs/40 km) for city sightseeing; Rs 1100 to include Srirangapatnam and Brindavan.

Train
Advance Computerized Reservations are dealt with in a separate section; ask for the 'foreigners' counter'. T131. Enquiries T0821-252 0103, 0800-2000 (closed 1330-1400); Sun 0800-1400. Left luggage 0600-2200, Rs 3-6 per day. Tourist information, telephone and toilets on Platform 1. Taxi counter at entrance. To **Bengaluru (Bangalore)** (non-stop): *Tipu Exp, 16205*, 1120, 2½ hrs; *Shatabdi Exp, 12008*, daily except Wed, 1415, 2 hrs (continues to **Chennai**, another 5 hrs). **Bengaluru** via **Srirangapatnam**, **Mandya** and **Maddur**: *Chamundi Exp 16215*, 0645, 3 hrs; *Kaveri Chennai Exp 16221*, 2015, 2¾ hrs. **Chennai**: *Chennai Exp 16221*, 2015, 10½ hrs; *Shatabdi Exp, 12008*, not Wed, 1415, 7 hrs. **Madurai**: change at Bengaluru. **Mumbai**: *Sharavathi Exp, 11036*, Sun only, 0630, 24 hrs.

Srirangapatnam → *Phone code: 08236. Population: 21,900. See map, page 44.*
The island is over 3 km long and 1 km wide so it's best to hire a bicycle from a shop on the main road to get around.

Srirangapatnam, 12 km from Mysore, has played a crucial role in the region since its origins in the 10th century. Occupying an easily fortified island site in the Kaveri River, it has been home to religious reformers and military conquerors. It makes a fascinating day trip from Mysore; Daria Daulat Bagh and the Gumbaz are wonderful.

The name Srirangapatnam comes from the **Temple of Sri Ranganathaswamy**, which stands aloof at the heart of the fortress, containing a highly humanistic idol of Lord Vishnu reclining on the back of a serpent. Dating from AD 894, it is far older than the fort and town, and was subsequently added to by the Hoysala and Vijayanagar kings. The latter built the fort in 1454, and occupied the site for some 150 years until the last Vijayanagar ruler handed over authority to the Hindu Wodeyars of Mysore, who made it their capital. In the second half of the 18th century it became the capital of Haidar Ali, who defended it against the Marathas in 1759, laying the foundations of his expanding power. He was succeeded by his son Tipu Sultan, who also used the town as his headquarters until Colonel Wellesley, the future Duke of Wellington, established his military reputation by defeating the 'Tiger of Mysore' in battle on 4 May 1799. Tipu died in exceptionally fierce fighting near the north gate of the fort; the place is marked by a simple monument. The fort had triple fortifications, but the British destroyed most of it.

Jama Masjid ⓘ *0800-1300, 1600-2000.* The mosque, which Tipu had built, has delicate minarets, and there are two Hindu **temples**, to Narasimha (17th century) and Gangadharesvara (16th century).

Daria Daulat Bagh (Splendour of the Sea) ⓘ *1 km east of the fort, Sat-Thu 0900-1700, foreigners Rs 100, Indians Rs 5.* Tipu's beautiful summer palace was built in 1784 and is set in a lovely garden. This social historical jewel has colourful frescoes of battle scenes between the French, British and Mysore armies, ornamental arches and gilded paintings on the teak walls and ceilings crammed with interesting detail. The west wall shows Haidar Ali and Tipu Sultan leading their elephant forces at the battle of Polilur (1780), inflicting a massive defeat on the British. As a result of the battle, Colonel Baillie – the defeated British commander – was held prisoner in Srirangapatnam for many years. The murals on the east walls show Tipu offering hospitality to neighbouring princes at various palace durbars. The small museum upstairs has 19th-century European paintings and Tipu's belongings.

Tip...
On the banks of the Cauvery just north of the Lal Bagh Palace is a jetty where six-seater coracles are available for river rides.

The Gumbaz ⓘ *3 km east, Sat-Thu 0800-1830, donation collected.* This is the family mausoleum, approached through an avenue of cypresses. Built by Tipu in memory of his father, the ornate white dome protects beautiful ivory-on-wood inlay and Tipu's tiger-stripe emblem, some swords and shields. Haider Ali's tomb is in the centre, his wife to the east and Tipu's own to the west.

Ranganathittu Bird Sanctuary

5 km upstream of Srirangapatnam, 0700-1800, foreigners Rs 300, Indians Rs 50, camera Rs 25, video Rs 250. Boats (0830-1330, 1430-1830), foreigners Rs 300, Indians Rs 50. Jun-Oct best. Mysore City Bus 126, or auto-rickshaw from Srirangapatnam. Guided boat trips from the jetty last 15-20 mins.

The riverine site of this sanctuary was established in 1975. Several islands, some bare and rocky, others larger and well wooded, provide excellent habitat for waterbirds, including the black-crowned night heron, Eurasian spoonbill and cormorants. Fourteen species of waterbirds use the sanctuary as a breeding

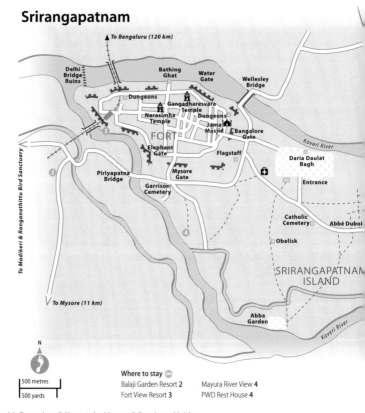

Srirangapatnam

To Bengaluru (120 km)

Delhi Bridge Ruins

Bathing Ghat

Water Gate

Wellesley Bridge

Dungeons

Gangadharesvara Temple

Narasimha Temple

Dungeons

Jama Masjid

Bangalore Gate

FORT

Kaveri River

Elephant Gate

Flagstaff

Daria Daulat Bagh

Piriyapatna Bridge

Mysore Gate

Entrance

Garrison Cemetery

To Madikeri & Ranganathittu Bird Sanctuary

Catholic Cemetery

Abbé Duboi

Obelisk

SRIRANGAPATNAM ISLAND

To Mysore (11 km)

Abba Garden

Kaveri River

N

500 metres
500 yards

Where to stay
Balaji Garden Resort **2**   Mayura River View **4**
Fort View Resort **3**   PWD Rest House **4**

ground from June onwards. There is a large colony of fruit bats in trees on the edge of the river and a number of marsh crocodiles between the small islands.

Somnathpur → *Phone code: 08227.*

This tiny village boasts the only complete Hoysala temple in the Mysore region. The drive east from Srirangapatnam via Bannur is particularly lovely, passing a couple of lakes through beautiful country and pretty, clean villages. The small but exquisite **Kesava Temple** (1268) ⓘ *0900-1700, foreigners Rs 100, Indians Rs 5, allow 1 hr, canteen, buses from Mysore take 1-1½ hrs; via Bannur (25 km, 45 mins) then to Somnathpur (3 km, 15 mins by bus, or lovely walk or bike ride through countryside),* is one of the best preserved of 80 Hoysala temples in this area. Excellent ceilings show the distinctive features of the late Hoysala style, and here the roof is intact where other famous temples have lost theirs. The temple has three sanctuaries with the *trikutachala* (triple roof) and stands in the middle of its rectangular courtyard (70 m long, 55 m wide) with cloisters containing 64 cells around it. From the east gateway is a superb view of the temple with an ambulatory standing on its raised platform, in the form of a 16-pointed star. The pillared hall in the centre with the three shrines to the west give it the form of a cross in plan. Walk around the temple to see the fine bands of sculptured figures. The lowest of the six shows a line of elephants, symbolizing strength and stability, then horsemen for speed, followed by a floral scroll. The next band of beautifully carved figures (at eye level) is the most fascinating and tells stories from the epics. Above is the *yali* frieze, the monsters and foliage possibly depicting the river Ganga and uppermost is a line of *hamsa*, the legendary geese.

Sivasamudram

80 km east of Mysore. Take a bus from Mysore or Bengaluru to Kollegala, then hire a taxi or autorickshaw.

Here, the Kaveri plunges over 100 m into a series of wild and inaccessible gorges. At the top of the falls the river divides around the island of Sivasamudram, the Barachukki channel on the east and the

Gaganchukki on the west. The hydroelectricity project was completed in 1902, the first HEP scheme of any size in India. It's best visited during the wet season, when the falls are an impressive sight, as water cascades over a wide area in a series of leaps.

Biligiri Rangaswamy Wildlife Sanctuary → *Altitude: 1000-1600 m.*

80 km south of Mysore, 0600-0900, 1600-1830, foreigners Rs 2400, Indians Rs 800. From Mysore, access is via Nanjangud (23 km) and Chamarajanagar, where there's a Forest Check Post. For information, contact Deputy Conservator of Forests, Sultan Sheriff Circle, Chamarajanagar, T08226-222059.

A hilly area with moist deciduous and semi-evergreen forests interspersed with grassland, the Biligiri Rangaswamy Hills represent a biodiversity crossroads between the eastern and western sides of the Ghats. Some of the largest elephant populations east of the divide occur here, along with sloth bear (better sightings here than at other southern sanctuaries), panther, elephant, deer, gaur and the occasional tiger, as well as 270 species of bird. The local Forest Department has recently begun offering treks through the sanctuary, guided by members of the tribal community. The best time for wildlife sighting is November to May. The local Soliga hill tribes pay special respect to an ancient champak tree (*Doddasampige mara*) believed to be 1000 years old and the abode of Vishnu.

Bandipur National Park → *Altitude: 780-1455 m. Area: 874 sq km.*

96 km southwest of Mysore. 0600-0900, 1530-1830, reception centre 0900-1630; Mysore–Ooty buses stop at the main entrance. Except for jeep safaris run by local lodges, the only access is by the Forest Department's uninspiring 1-hr bus safari: foreigners Rs 100, plus park entry fee of Rs 2400, Indians Rs 800. For information, contact Deputy Conservator of Forests, T08229-236043 (Mysore T0821-248 0901), dcfbandipur@yahoo.co.in.

Bandipur was set up by the Mysore maharaja in 1931, and now forms part of the Nilgiri Biosphere Reserve, sharing borders with Mudumalai National Park in Tamil Nadu and Kerala's Wayanad Wildlife Sanctuary. It has a mixture of subtropical moist and dry deciduous forests (principally teak and anogeissus) and scrubland in the Nilgiri foothills. The wetter areas support rosewood, silk cotton, sandalwood and *jamun*. You may spot gaur, chital (spotted deer), elephant, sambar, flying squirrel and four-horned antelope, but tigers and leopards are rare. There's also a good variety of birdlife including crested hawk, serpent eagles and tiny-eared owls.

Nagarhole (Rajiv Gandhi) National Park

50 km west of Mysore, 0600-0900, 1530-1830. Foreigners Rs 2400 per safari (by boat, jeep or bus), Indians Rs 800. Main entrance is at Karapur, on the Mysore–Mananthavady road, close to Kabini River Lodge and several other resorts. Another road enters the park near Hunsur on the northern side, where Deputy Conservator of Forests may grant permission for private jeep safaris and forest treks; enquire in advance on T08222-252064, dcfhunsur@rediffmail.com. Both roads across the park are closed after dusk to allow animal movements.

Nagarhole (meaning 'snake streams') was once the maharajas' reserved forest and became a national park in 1955. Covering gentle hills bordering Kerala, it's now one of India's greatest conservation successes, with predator populations at their maximum possible density and poaching virtually wiped out. The park's habitat range includes swampland, streams, moist deciduous forest, stands of bamboo and valuable timber in teak and rosewood trees. The Kabini River, which is a tributary of the Kaveri, flows through the forest where the upper canopy reaches 30 m. The park is accessible both by road and river. A number of tribesmen, particularly Kurumbas (honey gatherers) who still practise ancient skills, live amongst, and care for, the elephants.

In addition to elephants, the park also has gaur (Indian bison), dhole (Indian wild dogs), wild cats, four-horned antelopes, flying squirrels, sloth bears, monkeys and sambar deer. Tigers and leopards are hard to see except in the pre-monsoon summer, when dry conditions bring prey and predators to the few man-made waterholes. Many varieties of birds include the rare Malabar trogon, great black woodpecker, Indian pitta, pied hornbill, whistling thrush, green imperial pigeon and also waterfowl and reptiles.

The edge of the dam is the best place to view wildlife, particularly during the dry period from March to June, when elephants gather in their hundreds, and other herbivores in even greater numbers, to feast on vegetation left exposed by the receding dam waters.

The Forest Department runs two- to three-hour safaris in the morning and evening – currently the only way to explore the 'tourism' zone of the park, though local operators are campaigning to allow private safaris. Only a limited number of government jeeps are allowed into the park for each session, and to have a chance to get a slot you need to be staying at one of the resorts and lodges around Karapur.

Listings Around Mysore *map p44*

Srirangapatnam

$$ Mayura River View
Mysore Rd, T08236-217454.
Beautifully situated on the croc-filled river with 8 comfortable rooms (2 with a/c), sit-outs and a good vegetarian restaurant (Indian, Chinese). Very quiet and relaxing.

$$-$ Balaji Garden Resort
Mysore Rd (1 km from Piriyapatna Bridge), T08236-217355.

12 good-value cottages and 28 smallish rooms built with some style around a central courtyard. Rooms are well furnished, tiled and comfy; cottages are good value. There's a pool, restaurant.

$$-$ Fort View Resort
On the Bengaluru–Mysore road, T08236-252577.
12 upmarket rooms (4 with corner tub), Rajasthani architecture and huge beds, set in shady landscaped gardens. The restaurant is a little gloomy and

overpriced but there's an organic kitchen garden, pool, boating and fishing. Efficient.

$ PWD Rest House.
Book ahead at the PWD office near Ranganathaswami Temple, T08236-252051.
Charming former residence of George Harris. Basic rooms, but clean and quiet.

Biligiri Rangaswamy Wildlife Sanctuary
As in most Karnataka wildlife parks, the lodges and forest rest houses here charge foreigners double the rate Indians pay.

$$$ K Gudi Camp
Kyathadevara, book via Jungle Lodges, T080-2559 7025, www.junglelodges.com.
8 twin-bedded quality tents with modern toilets, or 4 rooms with 4 beds at the royal hunting lodge. Simple meals in the open air, elephant rides, birding, trekking. A comfortable experience despite the remoteness.

Bandipur National Park
Reserve rooms in advance; avoid weekends.

$$$ Bandipur Safari Lodge
At Melkamanahalli nearby, T080-4055 4055, www.junglelodges.com.
Simple rooms in cottages and a restaurant under shady trees. Rates include nature walks, park safaris and entry fees.

$$$ Dhole's Den
Kaniyanapura village, T08229-236062, www.dholesden.com.
Lovely small resort, with 2 rooms, a spacious suite and 2 large cottages, done out in modern minimalist style with a minimal-impact ethos: there's no TV or a/c, most electricity comes from wind turbines and solar, and you can pick your own veggies from the organic garden for dinner.

$ Venu Vihar Lodge
20 km from the park reception. Book in advance through the Forest Department, Woodyard, Mysore, T0821-248 0110.
Set in the beautiful Gopalaswamy Hills. Meals are available but take provisions.

Nagarhole
Safari lodges around Nagarhole are, with one notable exception, very expensive, though rates generally include jeep safaris. More affordable rooms are available in homestays around Kutta on the western fringe of the park. A 2-tier pricing structure operates in many lodges and hotels; where applicable, prices quoted are for foreigners.

$$$$ Kabini River Lodge
At Karapur on the reservoir bank, T080-2559 7025, www.junglelodges.com.
Accommodation consists of 14 rooms in a Mysore maharajas' 18th-century hunting lodge and bungalow, 6 newer cabins overlooking the lake or 5 tents, simple but acceptable. Good restaurant and bar, exchange facilities. The package includes meals, sailing, jeep/minibus at Nagarhole, and park tour with a naturalist. Very friendly and well run.

$$$$ Orange County Kabini
Bheeramballi Village, T08228-269100, www.orangecounty.in.
A long slow drive on rutted roads, or a short boat ride across the lake, brings you to this beautiful resort in a tree-shaded compound. Luxurious individual huts, built and furnished in a smart take on tribal style, come with private courtyard pool or spa. 2 restaurants,

and a beautiful reading room overlooking the lake, plus guided activities including coracle trips, elephant and bullock cart rides.

$$$ The Bison
1 km from the park gate in Gundathur village, T080-4127 8708, www.thebisonresort.com.
A wildlife camp in the truest sense, this rustic collection of lakeside tents and treehouses come with lashings of Victorian explorer style – hurricane lamps, antique 4-posters, and rickety gangplanks. Lodge owner Shaaz Jung is one of India's best young wildlife photographers, and a passionate and knowledgeable tracker, and a few days spent on safari with him may well represent your best chance in South India of spotting a leopard or tiger. Not luxurious, but superb value and most highly recommended.

$$$ Waterwoods
500 m from Kabini River Lodge, surrounded by the Kabini River, T08228-264421.
Exquisitely furnished ranch-style house, 6 luxury rooms with sit-outs, beautiful gardens on the water's edge, delicious home cooking, solar power, friendly staff, boating, jeep, Ayurvedic massage, gym, swimming and walking. Charming, informal atmosphere, peaceful, secluded.

Transport

Srirangapatnam
Trains and buses between **Bengaluru** and **Mysore** stop here but arrival can be tiresome with hassle from rickshaw drivers, traders and beggars. Buses 313 and 316 from Mysore **City Bus Stand** (half-hourly) take 50 mins.

Bandipur National Park
Bus
Bandipur and the neighbouring Mudumalai NP in Tamil Nadu are both on the Mysore to Ooty bus route, about 2½ hrs south from Mysore and 2½ hrs from Ooty. Buses go to and from **Mysore** (80 km) between 0615-1530.

Coorg, once a proud warrior kingdom, then a state, has now shrunk to become the smallest district in Karnataka. It is a beautiful anomaly in South India in that it has, so far, retained its original forests. Ancient rosewoods jut out of the Western Ghat hills to shade the squat coffee shrubs which the British introduced as the region's chief commodity. Like clockwork, 10 days after the rains come, these trees across whole valleys burst as one into white blossom drenching the moist air with their thick perfume, a hybrid of honeysuckle and jasmine. Although the climate is not as cool as other hill stations, Coorg's proximity by road to the rest of Karnataka makes it a popular weekend bolthole for inhabitants of Bengaluru. The capital of Coorg District, Madikeri, is an attractive small town in a beautiful hilly setting surrounded by the forested slopes of the Western Ghats and has become a popular trekking destination.

Madikeri (Mercara) → *Phone code: 08272. Population: 32,300. Altitude: 1150 m.*

The **Omkareshwara Temple**, dedicated to both Vishnu and Siva, was built in 1820. The tiled roofs are typical of Keralan Hindu architecture, while the domes show Muslim influence. On high ground dominating the town is the **fort** with its three stone gateways, built between 1812-1814 by Lingarajendra Wodeyar II. It has a small **museum** ⓘ *Tue-Sun 0900-1700, closed holidays*, in St Mark's Church as well as the town prison, a temple and a chapel while the palace houses government offices. The **Rajas' Tombs** (*Gaddige*), built in 1820 to the north of the town, are the memorials of Virarajendra and his wife and of Lingarajendra. Although the rajas were Hindu, their commemorative monuments are Muslim in style; Kodagas both bury and cremate their dead. The **Friday Market** near the bus stand is very colourful as all the local tribal people come to town to sell their produce. It is known locally as shandy, a British bastardization of the Coorg word *shante*, meaning market. On Mahadevped Road, which leads to the Rajas' tombs, is a 250-year-old **Siva temple** which has an interesting stone façade. Madikeri also has an attractive nine-hole golf course.

Essential Coorg (Kodagu)

Finding your feet

At present Coorg is only accessible by road, although an airport and railway station are planned. Frequent local and express buses arrive at Madikeri's bus stand from the west coast after a journey through beautiful wooded hills passing small towns and a wildlife sanctuary. From Mysore and Coimbatore an equally pleasant route traverses the Maidan. In winter there is often hill fog at night, making driving after dark dangerous. Madikeri is ideal for walking though you may need to hire an auto on arrival to reach the better hotels.

Around Madikeri

Madikeri and the surrounding area makes for beautiful walking but if you want to venture further you'll need to take a guide as paths can soon become indistinct and confusing.

Abbi Falls ⓘ *30-min rickshaw ride (9 km, Rs 150 round-trip).* The journey to the falls is through forests and coffee plantations. It is also an enjoyable walk along a fairly quiet road. The falls themselves are beautiful and well worth the visit. You can do a beautiful short trek down the valley and then up and around above the falls before rejoining the main road. Do not attempt it alone since there are no trails and you must depend on your sense of direction along forest paths. **Honey Valley Estate** (see page 54) has a book of walks around the guesthouse.

Bhagamandala ⓘ *36 km southwest, half-hourly service from Madikeri's private bus stand from 0630-2000, Rama Motors tour bus departs 0830, with 30-min stop.* At Bhagmandala the **Triveni bathing ghat** can be visited at the confluence of the three rivers: Kaveri, Kanike and Suiyothi. Among many small shrines the **Bhandeshwara Temple**, standing in a large stone courtyard surrounded by Keralan-style buildings on all four sides, is particularly striking. You can stay at the temple for a very small charge.

Madikeri

Kakkabe ⓘ *35 km south of Madikeri, bus from Madikeri to Kakkabe at 0630, jeep 1 hr.* Kakkabe is a small town, giving access to the highest peak in Coorg, **Thandiandamole** (1800 m). Nearby, **Padi Iggutappa** is the most important temple in Coorg.

Cauvery Nisargadhama ⓘ *0900-1800, Rs 150, still camera Rs 10.* This small island reserve in the Kaveri River is 2 km from Kushalnagar, accessed over a hanging bridge. Virtually untouched by tourism, it consists mostly of bamboo thickets and trees, including sandalwood, and is very good for seeing parakeets, bee eaters, woodpeckers and a variety of butterflies. There is a deer park, pedalo boating, a resident elephant and tall bamboo tree houses for wildlife viewing.

Bylakuppe ⓘ *6 km south of Kushalnagar.* Bylakuppe is home to a large Tibetan settlement, established in 1961. Apart from the cognitive dissonance of seeing Himalayan monks sipping from coconuts in steamy South India, the main point of interest here

N

Not to scale

Where to stay
Capitol Village **1**
Cauvery **2**
Chitra **3**
Hilltown **5**
Mayura Valley View **6**

Popular Residency **7**
Rajdarshan **10**
Vinayaka Lodge **9**

Restaurants
Choice **1**
East End **2**
Taj **3**
Taste of Coorg **4**
Udupi Veglands **5**

BACKGROUND
Coorg

Although there were references to the Kodaga people in the Tamil Sangam literature of the second century AD, the earliest Kodaga inscriptions date from the eighth century. After the Vjiayanagar Empire was defeated in 1565, many of their courtiers moved south, establishing regional kingdoms. One of these groups was the Haleri Rajas, members of the Lingayat caste whose leader Virarajendra set up the first Kodaga dynasty at Haleri, 10 km from the present district capital of Madikeri.

The later Kodagu Rajas were noted for some bizarre behaviour. Dodda Vira (1780-1809) was reputed to have put most of his relatives to death, a pattern followed by the last king, Vira Raja, before he was forced to abdicate by the British in 1834. In 1852 the last Lingayat ruler of Kodagu, Chikkavirarajendra Wodeyar, became the first Indian prince to sail to England, and the economic character of the state was quickly transformed. Coffee was introduced, becoming the staple crop of the region.

The forests of Kodagu are still home to wild elephants, which often crash into plantations on jackfruit raids, and other wildlife. The Kodaga, a tall, fair and proud landowning people who flourished under the British, are renowned for their martial prowess; almost every family has one member in the military. They also make incredibly warm and generous hosts – a characteristic you can discover thanks to the number of plantation homestays in inaccessible estates of dramatic beauty pioneered here following the crash in coffee prices. Kodagu also has a highly distinctive cuisine, in which *pandi* curry (pork curry) and *kadumbuttu* (rice dumplings) are particular favourites.

is the **Namdroling Monastery**, home to a community of 5000 lamas, where the Golden Temple houses beautiful murals and 60-foot high golden statues of the Buddha, Guru Padmasambhava, and Buddha Amitayus. A popular tourist destination on weekends, it's easy enough to visit for a day, but if you wish to stay in Bylakuppe you'll need to apply for an Inner Line Permit; see www.palyul.org.

Dubare Elephant Camp ⓘ *On the road between Kushalnagar and Siddapur, 0830-1200, 1630-1730, Rs 50, Indians Rs 20, plus Rs 200 each for riding, bathing and feeding elephant.* At this government-owned centre on the banks of the Kaveri you can feed and bathe elephants and line up for a short ride. The boat ride across the broad river is an appealing element of the experience in itself.

Tourist information

Tourist office
Mysore Rd, south of the Thinmaya statue, T08272-228580.

Coorg Wildlife Society
2 km further out on Mysore Rd, T08272-223505.
Can help with trekking advice and permits for catch-and-release *mahseer* fishing on the Kaveri River.

Where to stay

Madikeri
Power cuts are common so carry a torch and keep candles handy. Book early during holidays.

$$ Capitol Village
5 km southeast of town on Siddapur Rd, T08272-200135.
This traditional Keralan building (tiled roof and wooden beams) is set in a coffee, cardamom and pepper estate with a large pond. There are 13 large, airy rooms and a dorm (Rs 150). It's very quiet with excellent birdlife and outdoor eating under shady trees (Rs 75-150). A rickshaw from the centre costs Rs 100.

$$ Mayura Valley View (KSTDC)
Raja's Seat, T08272-228387, or book at Karnataka Tourism, Bengaluru, T080-2221 2901.
Perched on a cliff-top with stunning views especially at sunset. 25 clean and recently renovated rooms, and a pretty good restaurant. A cut above the usual government-run guesthouse.

$$-$ Chitra
School Rd, near the bus stand, T08272-225372, www.hotelchitra.com.
54 nondescript rooms, simple but clean, with Western toilets and hot showers. North Indian vegetarian restaurant, bar, helpful and knowledgeable English-speaking trekking guide (Mr Muktar).

$$-$ Rajdarshan, 116/2 MG Rd
T08272-229142, www.hotel rajdarshan.net.
Modern hotel with 25 well-laid-out clean rooms (in need of renovation) and an excellent restaurant. Staff are friendly and there are views over the town.

$ Cauvery
School Rd, T08272-225492.
26 clean, pleasant but basic rooms with fans, Indian meals, bar, away from the main road. Helpful management, information on trekking (stores luggage).

$ Hilltown
Daswal Rd, T08272-223801, hilltown@rediffmail.com.
38 modern, pleasant and airy rooms with TV in this new hotel with marble floors throughout and a restaurant. Great value. Highly recommended.

$ Popular Residency
Kohinoor Rd, T08272-221644.
New hotel with 10 clean and pleasant rooms, well fitted out, North Indian vegetarian restaurant, good value.

$ Vinayaka Lodge
25 m from the bus stand, T08272-229830.
50 rooms with bath, hot water buckets, friendly staff, clean and quiet (though the bus stand can be noisy in the early morning). Good value.

Around Madikeri

$$$$ Orange County
Karadigodu Post, Siddapur, T08274-258481, www.orangecounty.in.
One of the most beautiful resorts in all of South India, set on a working 300-acre coffee plantation.
63 cottages – some built of traditional red stone and dark timber, others decked out in modern style with high ceilings and big windows – all but 8 of which come with their own private pool. Warm and friendly staff, several good restaurants, and naturalist-led activities including excellent guided birdwatching and coracle rides on the Kaveri. Highly recommended.

$ Forest Rest House
Cauvery Nisargadhama, contact Forestry Office, Madikeri, T08272-228305, dfo_madikeri@yahoo.com.
11 simple cottages built largely of bamboo and teak, some with balconies on stilts over the water, electricity (no fan), hot water, peaceful (despite nocturnal rats), but poor food.

$ Honey Valley Estate
Yavakapadi, Kakkabe, 3 km up a track only a jeep can manage, T08272-238339, www.honeyvalleyindia.in.
This place has less stunning views than the **Palace Estate** (the house is screened by tall trees) but equally good access by foot to trekking trails. Facilities are mostly better and it can fit over 30 guests. The host family is charming too. Also has a hut 2 km into the forest for those wanting more isolation.

$ Palace Estate
2 km south of Kakkabe (Rs 70 in a rickshaw) along Palace Rd, T08272-238446, www.palaceestate.co.in.

A small, traditional farm growing coffee, pepper, cardamom and bananas lying just above the late 18th-century Nalnad Palace, a summer hunting lodge of the kings of Coorg. The 6 basic rooms with shared veranda have a 180° panorama of forested hills all the way to Madikeri. Isolated and an excellent base for walking; Coorg's highest peak is 6 km from the homestay. Home-cooked local food, English-speaking guide Rs 150.

Restaurants

Madikeri

$ Capitol
Near Private Bus Stand.
Despite its exterior, serves excellent vegetarian fare.

$ Choice
School Rd.
Wide menu, very good food, choice of ground floor or rooftop dining.

$ East End
Gen Thimaya Rd.
Good old-fashioned restaurant, serving excellent *dosas*.

$ Taj
College Rd.
'Cheap and best', clean and friendly.

$ Taste of Coorg
CMC Building, near Town Hall.
The best place for traditional Coorgi delicacies like pork curry with *kadumbuttu* (steamed, ghee-laden rice balls).

$ Udupi Veglands
Opposite the fort.
Lovely, clean, spacious wooden eatery, delicious and cheap vegetarian *thalis*.

What to do

Madikeri
Fishing
Coorg Wildlife Society, *see page 53.*
Arranges licences for fishing on the
Kaveri River (Rs 500 per day, Rs 1000
weekend). The highlight is the prospect
of pulling in a *mahseer*, up to 45 kg in
weight; all fish must be returned to the
river. Fishing takes place at Trust Land
Estate, Valnoor, near Kushalnagar, where
there is a lodge; you'll need to bring your
own food.

Trekking
Friends' Tours and Travel, *below Bank
of India, College Rd, T08272-229974.*
Recommended for their knowledge and
enthusiasm. Tailor-made treks Rs 275 per
person per day including guide, food and
accommodation in temples, schools, etc.
A base camp is at Thalathmane, 4 km
from Madikeri, which people can also
stay at even if not trekking. Basic huts and
blankets for Rs 50 each, home cooking
available nearby at little extra cost.
Hotel Cauvery, *see page 53.* Also
arranges treks.

Transport

Madikeri
Auto-rickshaw
From **Hotel Chitra** to **Abbi Falls**, Rs 150
return, including a 1-hr wait at the falls.

Bus
From **KSRTC Bus Stand**, T08272-229134,
frequent express buses to **Bengaluru**,
Plat 4, from 0615 (6 hrs); **Chikmagalur**
(6 hrs); **Hassan** (3½ hrs); **Kannur** (4-5 hrs);
Mangalore, Plat 2, 0530-2400 (3½ hrs);

Mysore, Plat 3, half-hourly 0600-2300
(3 hrs) via **Kushalnagar** (for Tibetan
settlements), very crowded during the
rush hour (4 hrs); and **Thalassery**. Daily
to **Coimbatore, Madurai, Mumbai,
Ooty, Virajpet**.
   Private Bus Stand: **Kamadenu
Travels**, above bus stand, T08272-
225524, for **Purnima Travels** bus to
Bengaluru. **Shakti Motor Service**
to **Nagarhole** (4½ hrs).

Train
The closest stations are Mysore (120 km),
Hassan (130 km) and Mangalore (135 km).
Computerized reservations office on
Main Rd, T08272-225002, Mon-Sat 1000-
1700, Sun 1000-1400.

Around Madikeri
The bus from Madikeri to
Nisargadhama passes park gates 2 km
before Kushalnagar. A rickshaw from
Kushalnagar costs Rs 40.

Nagarhole
Bus
From **Mysore**, Mananthavady-bound
buses pass through **Karapur** (3 hrs),
though you'll need to arrange in
advance for your lodge to pick you
up. (You can get a cheap look at the
Nagarhole forest by catching the bus
all the way through to Mananthavady.)
Madikeri, 4½ hrs. **Bengaluru**, 6 hrs.
Jungle Lodges, T080-2559 7021,
www.junglelodges.com, buses leave
Bengaluru at 0730, stop in Mysore
(around 0930), reaching Kabini around
1230; return bus departs 1315.

Train
The nearest station is Mysore (96 km).

Western
Plateau

The world's tallest monolith – that of the Jain saint Gommateshwara – has stood majestic, 'skyclad' and lost in meditation high on Sravanabelagola's Indragiri hill since the 10th century. It is a profoundly spiritual spot, encircled by long sweeps of paddy and sugar cane plains, and is one of the most popular pilgrimage points for practitioners of the austere Jain religion. Some male Jain followers of the Digambar or skyclad sect of the faith climb the rock naked to denote their freedom from material bonds. Nearby lie the 11th- and 12th-century capital cities of Halebid and Belur, the apex of Hoysala temple architecture whose walls are cut into friezes of the most intricate soapstone. These villages of the Central Maidan sit in what has been the path of one of the main routes for trade and military movement for centuries.

Sravanabelagola, Belur and Halebid can all be seen in a very long day from Bengaluru, but it's far better to stay overnight near the sights themselves. Hotels in the temple villages tend to be very basic; for more comfortable options look towards the relaxed coffee-growing hill station of Chikmagalur, or Hassan, a pleasant, busy and fast-developing little city.

Hassan

Most visitors do little more than pass through Hassan en route to better things, taking advantage of its good range of hotels and transport connections. The city's main claim to fame is as home to the sinister-sounding Master Control Facility, one of two centres (the other is in Bhopal) responsible for controlling all of India's geostationary satellites.

Belur

Daily 0600-2000, but some temples close 1300-1600; free; carry a torch, ASI-trained guides on-site (often excellent), Rs 200 for 4 visitors, though official rate is higher.

Belur, on the banks of the Yagachi River, was the Hoysala dynasty's first capital and continues to be a significant town that is fascinating to explore. The gloriously elaborate Krishna Chennakesavara Temple was built over the course of a century from 1116 as a fitting celebration of the victory over the Cholas at Talakad.

Chennakesava Temple At first glance Chennakesava Temple (see also Somnathpur, page 45) appears unimpressive because the super-structure has been lost. However, the walls are covered with exquisite friezes. A line of 644 elephants (each different) surrounds the base, with rows of figures and foliage above. The detail of the 38 female figures is perfect. Look at the young musicians and dancers on either side of the main door and the unusual perforated screens between the columns. Ten have typical bold geometrical patterns while

Essential Western Plateau

Finding your feet

Hassan is the main transport hub in the area and a good base for visiting the Western Plateau temples. It has train and direct bus connections with Mysore (three hours) and Bengaluru (4½ hours). There are local buses from Hassan to Halebid, Belur and Sravanabelagola. Alternatively, taxis charge around Rs 1000 for a day tour.

In the Central Maidan, both Chitra-durga and Belgaum have bus and train stations with good connections.

Best place to stay...

Hoysala Village Resort, Hassan, page 60
The Serai, Chikmagalur, page 61
Taj Gateway, Chikmagalur, page 62

the other 10 depict scenes from the *Puranas* in their tracery. Inside superb carving decorates the hand lathe-turned pillars and the bracket-figures on the ceiling. Each stunning filigree pillar is startlingly different in design, a symptom of the intensely competitive climate the sculptors of the day were working in. The **Narasimha pillar** at the centre of the hall is particularly fine and originally could be rotated. The detail is astounding. The jewellery on the figures is hollow and movable and the droplets of water seem to hang at the ends of the dancer's wet hair on a bracket above you. On the platform in front of the shrine is Santalesvara dancing in homage to Lord Krishna. The shrine holds a 3-m-high black polished deity, occasionally opened for *darshan*. The annual **Car Festival** is held in March-April.

Viranarayana Temple West of **Chennakesava**, Viranarayana Temple has some fine sculpture and smaller shrines around it. The complex is walled with an ambulatory. The entrance is guarded by the winged figure of Garuda, Vishnu's carrier, who faces the temple with joined palms.

Halebid
Open daily 0700-1730, free.

The ancient capital of the Hoysala Empire was founded in the early 11th century. It was destroyed by the armies of the Delhi sultanate in 1311 and 1327. The great Hoysalesvara Temple, still incomplete after the best part of a century's toil, survived but the capital lay deserted and came to be called Halebid (ruined village), a name it continues to live up to.

Detour 1 km south to walk around the **Basthalli Garden** filled with remarkably simple 12th-century Jain Bastis. These have lathe-turned and multi-faceted columns, dark interiors and carved ceilings. The smaller **Kedaresvara Temple** with some highly polished columns is on a road going south. There are cycles for hourly hire to visit these quieter sites.

Hoysalesvara Temple The temple set in lawns has two shrines dedicated to Siva with a Nandi bull facing each. The largest of the Hoysala temples, it was started in 1121 but remains unfinished. It is similar in structure to Belur's, but its super-structure was never completed. Belur's real treats are in its interiors, while Halebid's are found on the outside reliefs. Six bands circle the star-shaped temple, elephants, lions, horsemen, a floral scroll and stories from the epics and the *Bhagavata Purana*. This frieze relates incidents from the *Ramayana* and *Mahabharata*; among them Krishna lifting Mount Govardhana and Rama defeating the demon god Ravana. The friezes above show *yalis* and *hamsa* or geese. There are exceptional half life-size deities with minute details at intervals. Of the original 84 female figures (like the ones at Belur) only 14 remain; thieves have made off with 70 down the centuries.

Archaeological Museum ⓘ *Sat-Thu 1000-1700, Rs 5, no photography.* The museum is on the lawn near the south entrance and has a gallery of 12th- to 13th-

Temples of Belur and Halebid

The Hoysalas, whose kingdom stretched between the Krishna and Kaveri rivers, encouraged competition among their artisans; their works even bear 12th-century autographs. Steatite (soapstone) meant that sculptors could fashion doily-like detail from solid rock since it is relatively soft when fresh from the quarry but hardens on exposure to air. The temples, built as prayers for victory in battle, are small but superb.

century sculptures, woodcarvings, idols, coins and inscriptions. Some sculptures are displayed outside. To the west is a small lake.

Sravanabelagola → *Phone code: 08176*

The ancient Jain statue of Gommateshwara stands on Vindhyagiri Hill (sometimes known as Indrabetta or Indragiri), 150 m above the plain; Chandragiri Hill to the north (also known as Chikka Betta) is just under half that height. The 17-m-high Gommateshwara statue, erected somewhere between AD 980 and AD 983, is of the enlightened prince Bahubali, son of the first Tirthankara (or holy Jain teacher). The prince won a fierce war of succession over his brother, Bharata, only to surrender his rights to the kingdom to take up a life of meditation.

In the town itself is the **Bhandari Basti** (1159, with later additions), about 200 m to the left from the path leading up to the Gommateshwara statue. Inside are 24 images of Tirthankaras in a spacious sanctuary. There are 500 rock-cut steps to the top of the hill that take half an hour to climb. It is safe to leave luggage at the tourist office at the entrance.

Vindhyagiri Hill You'll have to clamber barefoot up over 700 hot steep granite steps that carve up the hill to reach the statue from the village tank (socks, sold on-site, offer protection from the hot stone; take water), or charter a *dhooli* (a cane chair tied between two poles and carried), to let four bearers do the work for you. The small, intricately carved shrines you pass on the way up are the **Odeagal Basti**, the **Brahmadeva Mandapa**, the **Akhanda Bagilu** and the **Siddhara Basti**, all 12th-century except the Brahmadeva Mandapa which is 200 years older.

The carved **statue of Gommateshwara** is nude (possibly as he is a *Digambara* or 'sky-clad' Jain) and captures the tranquillity typical of Buddhist and Jain art. The depth of the saint's meditation and withdrawal from the world is suggested by the spiralling creepers shown growing up his legs and arms, and by the ant hills and snakes at his feet. Although the features are finely carved, the overall proportions are odd: he has huge shoulders and elongated arms but stumpy legs.

The 'magnificent anointment' (or **Mastakabhisheka**) falls every 12th year when Jain pilgrims flock from across India to bid for 1008 *kalashas* (pots) of holy water that are left overnight at the saint's feet. The next morning their contents, followed with ghee, milk, coconut water, turmeric paste, honey, vermilion powder and a dusting of gold, are poured over the saint's head from specially erected scaffolding. Unusually for India, the thousands of devotees watching the event do so in complete silence. The next celebration is in 2017.

Chandragiri Hill There are 14 shrines on Chandragiri Hill and the Mauryan emperor Chandragupta, who is believed by some to have become a Jain and left his empire to fast and meditate, is buried here. The temples are all in the Dravidian style, the **Chamundaraya Basti**, built in AD 982 being one of the most remarkable. There is a good example of a free-standing pillar or *mana-stambha* in front of the **Parsvanathasvami Basti**. These pillars, sometimes as high as 15 m, were placed at the temple entrance. Here, the stepped base with a square cross section transforms to a circular section and the column is then topped by a capital.

Chikmagalur (Chikkamagaluru)
Northeast of Belur, Chikmagalur sits at the centre of one of the country's most important coffee-growing areas. Coffee was first smuggled from Mocha (Yemen) to India in 1670 by the Sufi saint Baba Budan, after whom the surrounding Baba Budangiri Hills are named, and the **Central Coffee Research Institute** was set up here in 1925. Chikmagalur is now a popular weekend destination from Bengaluru, with scores of plantation 'homestays'. There are excellent views from the top of **Mulayanagiri** (1930 m), reached by a motorable road. Chikmagalur town has the Hoysala-style **Kodandarama Temple**, a number of mosques and a moated fort.

Listings Western Plateau temples

Tourist information

Tourist office
Vartha Bhavan, BM Rd, Sravanabelagola, T08172-268862. Closes 1300-1415.
Very helpful and can look after your bags while you climb the hill.

Where to stay

Hotels in Belur, Halebid and Sravanabelagola have only basic facilities, but allow you to see these rural towns and villages before or after the tour groups. Due to the climb, Sravanabelagola particularly benefits from an early start. Hassan and Chikmagalur are more comfortable.

Hassan

$$$ Hotel Southern Star
BM Rd, T08172-251816, www.ushalexushotels.com.
Large modern hotel with 48 excellent a/c rooms, hot water, phone, satellite TV, and great views across the town and countryside. Excellent service.

$$$ Hoysala Village Resort
Belur Rd, 6 km from Hassan, T08172-256764, www.trailsindia.com.
33 big cottage rooms with hot water, TV, tea and coffee maker and fan, are spread out across this landscaped, bird-filled resort. It's rustic, with small handicraft shops, a good restaurant and swimming pool and very attentive service.

$$$-$$ The Ashhok Hassan (ITDC)
BM Rd, 500 m from the bus stand, T08172-268731, www.hassanashok.com.
Dramatic renovation has created 36 lovely rooms in this immaculate, soundproofed hotel in central Hassan. Decor is all about clean lines and modern art, and facilities include all mod cons from a/c to Wi-Fi. Charming suites have big rattan armchairs; the Hoysaleshara suite has its own dining room, bar and steam bath. Excellent service and tidy garden with pool.

$$-$ Hotel Sri Krishna
BM Rd, T08172-263240.
40 rooms with hot water 0600-1000, TV, some with a/c, also double-bedded twin suites for 4 and a dorm for 10. There's a busy South Indian restaurant with plantain leaf service, and car hire. Good value.

$$-$ Hotel Suvarna Regency
97 BM Rd, 500 m south of the bus stand, T08172-264006.
70 clean, big a/c rooms, some with bath. It's a bit musty but the deluxe and suite rooms are nice. There's a good vegetarian restaurant and car hire available. Very helpful. Also has 4- to 6-bed dorms and triples.

Belur

$ Mayura Velapuri (KSTDC)
Temple Rd, T08177-222209.
Reasonably clean and spacious rooms including 6 doubles, 4 triples and 2 dorms sleeping 20 (Rs 75 per person), with hot water and fan. There's a TV and sitting areas. Friendly staff. Good South Indian meals served in the restaurant.

$ Vishnu Regency
Main Rd, T08177-223011, vishnuregency_belur@yahoo.co.in.
20 clean rooms opening onto a courtyard, some with TV and fan, and hot water in the morning. It's a welcoming hotel with a shop and good veg restaurant serving tandoor, curries and *thalis*.

Halebid

$ Mayura Shantala (KSTDC)
T08177-273224.
Inspection Bungalow compound in a nice garden overlooking the temple. There are 4 twin-bed tiled rooms with fan, nets and bath, and a kitchen.

Sravanabelagola
The temple Management Committee (SDJMI), T08176-257258, can help organize accommodation in basic pilgrim hostels. Check in the **SP Guest House** by the bus stand.

$ Raghu
Near the base of the steps up to Indragiri, T08176-257238.
Small and utterly basic but clean rooms above a decent veg restaurant.

$ Vidyananda Nilaya Dharamshala
Closest to the bus stand, reserve through SDJMI.
Rooms with toilet and fan, bucket baths, blanket but no sheets, courtyard. Good value.

Chikmagalur

$$$$ The Serai
7 km from town on the Kadur-Mangalore Rd, T08262-224903, www.theserai.in.
Fabulously luxurious new resort owned by the **Coffee Day** café chain, with beautiful and very private villas cascading down the hill among coffee and pepper bushes. Everything's designed on clean lines, the villas come

with private pools, and service is discreet and efficient. There's a spa, billiard room, and daily plantation tours. Popular with visiting cricketers and movie stars.

$$$ Gateway
*KM Rd, T08262-660660,
www.thegatewayhotels.com.*
29 luxury a/c rooms lined along the pool, superb staff and food, a good base for visiting Belur and Halebid (40 km).

Restaurants

Hassan
The veg restaurant and multi-cuisine **Suvarna Gate** at **Hotel Suvarna Regency** are the best in town. The restaurant at **Hotel Sri Krisha** is also popular, while the restaurants attached to **Hassan Ashhok**, **Hoysala Village** and **Southern Star** are best for those worried about hygiene. See Where to stay.

$ GRR
Opposite the bus stand.
For non-veg food and friendly staff.

Belur
This sizeable town has numerous tea shops and vegetarian stands. **Vishnu Regency Hotel** (see Where to stay) has the best tourist restaurant.

Transport

Hassan
Bus
For local buses, T08172-268418. Long-distance buses at least hourly to **Belur** from about 0700 (35 km, 1 hr) and **Halebid** from about 0800 (31 km, 1 hr); very crowded. Few direct to **Sravanabelagola** in the morning (1 hr); alternatively, travel to **Channarayapatna** and change to bus for Sravanabelagola.

Also to **Bengaluru** about every 30 mins (4½ hrs), **Goa** (14 hrs), **Mangalore** (5 hrs), **Mysore** hourly (3 hrs). If heading for Hampi, you can reserve seats for the 0730 bus to **Hospet** (9 hrs).

Taxi
Taxis charge around Rs 1000 for a day-tour to **Halebid** and **Belur**, and the same for a trip to **Sravanabelagola**. Drivers park up along AVK College Rd near the bus stand.

Train
The railway station is 2 km east of centre, T08172-268222, with connections to **Bengaluru**, **Mysore** and **Mangalore**.

Belur
Bus
The bus stand is about 1 km from the temples. Buses run half-hourly to **Hassan** (1 hr; last at 2030) and **Halebid** (30 mins). Also to **Shimoga**, where you can change for **Hampi** and **Jog Falls** (4 hrs); and to **Mysore** (1½ hrs).

Halebid
Bus
The bus stand, where you can get good meals, is near the temples. KSRTC buses run half-hourly to **Hassan** (45 mins) and from there to **Bengaluru**, **Mangalore**, **Mysore**. Also direct to **Belur** (12 km, 30 mins).

Sravanabelagola
Bus
Direct buses to/from **Mysore** and **Bengaluru** run in the morning; in the afternoon, change at **Channarayapatna**. The morning express buses to/from Mysore serve small villages travelling over dusty but interesting roads up to Krishnarajapet, then very few stops between there and Mysore.

border region with an impressive fort complex

Chitradurga

At the foot of a group of granite hills rising to 1175 m in the south, is Chitradurga, 202 km northwest of Bengaluru. The **Fort of Seven Rounds** ⓘ *2 km from the bus stand, 4 km from the railway station, open sunrise to sunset, closed public holidays, Rs 100, allow 2 hrs*, was built in the 17th century by Nayak Poligars, semi-independent landlords who fled south after the collapse of the Vijayanagar Empire in 1565. They were crushed by Haidar Ali in 1779 who replaced the Nayaka's mud fort with stone and Tipu Sultan built a palace, mosque, granaries and oil pits in it. There are four secret entrances in addition to the 19 gateways and ingenious water tanks which collected rainwater. There are also 14 temples, including a cave temple to the west of the wall. They are placed in an extraordinary jumble of granite outcrops, a similar setting to that of Hampi 300 km to the north. The **Hidimbeshwara Temple** is the oldest temple on the site.

Belgaum (Belagavi) → *Phone code: 0831. Population: 399,600.*

An important border town, Belgaum makes an interesting stop on the Mumbai–Bengaluru road or as a trip from Goa. The crowded market in the centre gives a glimpse of India untouched by tourism. With its strategic position in the Deccan Plateau, the town had been ruled by many dynasties including the Chalukyas, Rattas, Vijaynagaras, Bahmanis and the Marathas. Most of the monuments date from the early 13th century. The **fort**, immediately east of the town centre, though originally pre-Muslim, was rebuilt by Yusuf Adil Shah, the Sultan of Bijapur, in 1481. Inside, the **Masjid-i-Sata** (1519), the best of the numerous mosques in Belgaum, was built by a captain in the Bijapur army, Azad Khan. Belgaum is also noted for its Jain architecture and sculpture. The late **Chalukyan Kamala Basti**, with typical beautifully lathe-turned pillars and a black stone Neminatha sculpture, stands within the fort walls. To the south of the fort and about 800 m north of the **Hotel Sanman** on the Mumbai-Bengaluru bypass, is a beautifully sculpted **Jain temple** which, according to an inscription, was built by Malikaryuna.

Listings Central Maidan

Where to stay

Chitradurga

$$-$ Amogha International
Santhe Honda Rd, T08194-220763.
Clean, spacious and modern rooms and some a/c suites. 2 restaurants, good vegetarian, but the service is slow. The best place to stay in town.

$ Mayura Santhe Bagilu
Within the city walls, T08194-224448.
26 acceptable rooms, some with a/c and TV; it can be a bit noisy.

Belgaum
Hotels are mostly on College Rd and PB Rd.

$$-$ Adarsha Palace
College Rd, T0831-243 5777,
www.hoteladarshapalace.com.
Small, modern and personal hotel
with some a/c rooms and the excellent
Angaan vegetarian restaurant (rooftop
non-vegetarian). It's good value and
there's a pleasant atmosphere with
friendly staff. Recommended.

$$-$ Sanman Deluxe
College St, T0831-243 0777,
www.hotelsanman.org.
Similar to **Adarsha Palace**, in a new
building (much cheaper in the old
Sanman), 2 restaurants.

$ Keerthi
On the Pune–Bengaluru Rd, a short
walk from the Central Bus Stand, T0831-
246 6999.
A large modern hotel with some a/c
rooms and a restaurant.

$ Mayura Malaprabha (KSTDC)
Ashok Nagar, T0831-247 0781.
6 simple clean rooms in modern
cottages, or a dorm (Rs 40). There's a
restaurant, bar and tourist office on site.

$ Milan
Club Rd, 4 km from the train station,
T0831-242 5555.
45 rooms with bath (hot shower),
some with a/c, vegetarian restaurant,
good value.

$ Sheetal
Khade Bazar near bus station,
T0831-242 9222.
Noisy Indian-style hotel in a busy and
quite entertaining bazar street. Clean-ish
rooms with bath, vegetarian restaurant.

Restaurants

Belgaum

$ Gangaprabha
Kirloskar Rd.
Recommended for pure-veg food.

$ Zuber Biryaniwala
Kaktives Rd.
For creamy biryanis and good
non-veg curries.

Transport

Chitradurga
Bus
Buses to/from **Bengaluru**, **Davangere**,
Hospet, **Hubli** and **Mysore**.

Train
Train from **Arsikere**, **Bengaluru**,
Guntakal, **Hubli**.

Belgaum
Bus
Long-distance buses leave from the
Central Bus Stand, T0831-246 7932,
to **Panaji** (0600-1715), **Margao** (0545-
1500), **Mapusa** (0715-1715).

Train
The train station is near the bus stand,
4 km south of the centre; autos available
Bengaluru: *Ranichennamma Exp, 6590,*
1810, 13 hrs. **Mumbai** (**CST**) and **Pune**:
change at Pune for Mumbai *Chalukya/*
Sharavathi Exp, 1018/1036, Mon, Tue, Fri,
Sat, 1805, 14 hrs. **Goa** via **Londa** 8 trains
daily, 0135-2030, 1 hr.

West coast

pristine beaches, pilgrimage villages and bird-filled forests

Despite being sandwiched between the holiday honeypots of Goa and south Kerala, and despite having been given a glittering new name by the tourist board, Karnataka's 'Sapphire Coast' has thus far been slow to attract tourists. Yet the landscapes here are dreamy, riven by broad mangrove-lined creeks and carpeted with neon green paddy fields, and the beaches retain a wild beauty, almost entirely innocent of the joys and perils of banana pancakes, necklace hawkers and satellite TV.

The hilly port town of Mangalore makes a pleasant, relaxing stop between Goa and Kerala, but the jewel in the Sapphire Coast's crown thus far is undoubtedly Gokarna: a hippy stronghold, mass pilgrimage site and tremendously sacred Hindu centre. It's little more than one narrow street lined with traditional wooden houses and temples, but it is packed with pilgrims and has been adopted, along with Hampi, by the Goa overspill: people lured by spirituality and the beautiful, auspiciously shaped Om Beach. The no-frills hammock and beach hut joints of yore have now been joined by the snazzy, eco-conscious CGH Earth's well-regarded boutique yoga hotel, SwaSwara, based on the Bihar school.

Essential West coast

Finding your feet

Mangalore is the main transport hub for the region with an international airport 22 km north, as well as frequent bus and train connections with most towns and cities. Buses ply the Sapphire Coast, with regular connections from Mangalore to Gokarna (five hours). Two train lines serve the region. The Konkan railway carries trains from Mumbai via Goa to Mangalore, while the broad-gauge line goes down the coast to destinations in Kerala, inland Karnataka and Tamil Nadu.

Mangalore is the main service town with several banks and internet cafés. Gokarna is well set up for tourists though facilities are low-key and basic, especially on the beach.

Best places to stay...

Old Magazine House, page 76
SwaSwara, page 76

When to go

October to March is best. The Deccan Plateau and the coast are intensely hot in April and May, with humidity building up as the monsoon approaches. The roads between Mangalore and the Deccan Plateau, and some of the coastal roads, are badly affected by the monsoon rains and become very potholed. Jog Falls are at their best from late November to early January.

Set on the banks of the Netravathi and Gurupur rivers, the friendly capital of South Kanara District is rarely explored by Western tourists, but Mangalore offers some interesting churches and temples and makes a worthy stopping point on your way between beaches. An important shipbuilding centre during Haider Ali's time, it is now a major port exporting coffee, spices and cashew nuts.

Sights

St Aloysius College Chapel ⓘ *Lighthouse Hill, 0830-1300, 1600-2000*, has remarkable 19th-century frescoes painted by the Italian-trained Jesuit priest Moscheni, which cover the walls and ceilings in a profusion of scenes. The town has a sizeable Roman Catholic population (about 20%). The nearby **Old Lighthouse** in Tagore Park was built by Haider Ali.

The tile-roofed low structure of the 10th-century **Mangaladevi Temple** ⓘ *south of the Central train station, bus 27 or 27A, 1600-1200, 1600-2000*, is named after a Malabar Princess, Mangala Devi, who may have given her name to Mangalore.

The 11th-century **Sri Manjunatha Temple** ⓘ *4 km northeast of the centre in the Kadri Hills, 0600-1300, 1600-*

Tip...

The centre of Mangalore is compact enough to be covered on foot but auto-rickshaws are handy for longer journeys. Most refuse to use their meters so ask locally what the fare should be.

2000, Rs 30-40 by auto, has a rough lingam; its central image is a superb bronze Lokeshwara made in AD 968, said to be one of the finest in South India.

Sreemanthi Bai Memorial Museum ① *just north of the KSRTC Bus Station, 0900-1700, free*, has a collection including archaeology, ethnology, porcelain and woodcarvings.

Mangalore

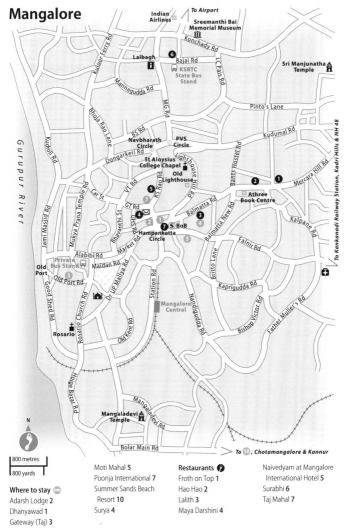

South of the Netravathi River lies **Ullal**, which has a pleasant beach and the *dargah* of **Sayyed Mohammed Shareefulla Madani**, a Sufi saint who sailed here from Medina in the 16th century. The *dargah* itself was built in the 19th century, and is credited with healing powers: You can take a trip out to the sand bar at the river mouth to watch fascinating boat building and river traffic on the Netravathi River.

Around Mangalore

The forested hills of the Western Ghats are home to some wonderful examples of Jain and Hindu sculpture and architecture, easily visited on a long day's excursion from Mangalore or as a break on the journey to Belur and Halebid (see pages 57 and 58). The temples are often centres of pilgrimage, such as the **Subrahmanya Temple** at **Sullia** and the Shaivite **Manjunatha Temple** at **Dharmasthala**; the latter, 70 km inland, receives thousands of pilgrims every day. From here you can head north through **Venur**, with a 12-m monolith of Bahubali built in 1605, to **Karkala**, where the Bahubali statue is second in height only to that of Sravanabelagola (see page 59); the **Mastabhisheka ceremony** is performed here every 12 years (next scheduled for 2014). Further northeast is the small town of **Sringeri**, near the source of the Tunga River, which is associated with the Hindu philosopher Sankaracharya. South of Karkala lies **Mudabidri**, the 'Jain Varanasi', with a collection of superbly carved *basti*. In Jain tradition, no two columns are alike, and many are elaborately carved with graceful figures and floral and knot patterns.

Listings Mangalore *map p67*

Tourist information

Main tourist office
City Corporation Building, Lalbagh, just west of the KSRTC Bus Stand, Mangalore, T0824-245 3926. Open 1000-1730.

Where to stay

$$$ Gateway (Taj)
Old Port Rd, T0824-666 0420, www.tajhotels.com.
87 excellent rooms and 6 spacious suites, some with sea/river view. Good facilities including a restaurant and pool. Friendly service.

$$$ Summer Sands Beach Resort
Ullal Beach, 10 km south of town, T0824-246 7690, www.summer-sands.com.

85 rooms, 30 of which are a/c, in simple but comfortable local-style bungalows. Superb Konkani meals available, as well as a bar, good pool, Ayurvedic treatments, yoga and local trips.

$$-$ Moti Mahal
Falnir Rd, T0824-244 1411, www.motimahalmangalore.com.
Tired-looking on the outside, but the 90 rooms and suites are comfortable and fresh. Excellent pool and health club (non-residents Rs 120), decent Chinese and Indian restaurants and a poolside barbecue.

$$-$ Poonja International
KS Rao Rd, T0824-244 0171, www.hotelpoonjainternational.com.
154 rooms, central a/c, with a wide range of facilities including currency exchange. It's spotlessly clean and

the price includes an excellent buffet breakfast. Great value.

$ Adarsh Lodge
Market Rd, T0824-244 0878.
60 basic but well-kept rooms with bath, some with TV. Staff are friendly and the service is excellent. Good value especially for singles.

$ Dhanyawad
Hampankatta Circle, T0824-244 0066.
44 spacious rooms, not the quietest location but the non-a/c doubles are huge for the price.

$ Surya
Greens Compound, Balmatta Rd, T0824-242 5736.
3 floors of uninspiring but adequate rooms with bath in a popular backpacker hotel, set back from road in a tranquil tree-shaded compound. Friendly and helpful management.

Restaurants

$$ Froth on Top
Balmatta Rd.
Convivial pub, serving a good range of beers and beer-friendly snacks.

$ Hao Hao
Bridge Rd, Balmatta.
Fun old-school Chinese restaurant dishing out mountain-sized bowls of fried noodles.

$ Lalith
Balmatta Rd.
Basement restaurant with excellent non-veg and seafood, cold beer and friendly service.

$ Maya Darshini
GHS Rd.
Succulent veg biryanis and great North Indian fare, plus interesting local breakfasts such as rice balls and *goli baje* (fried dough balls with chutney).

$ Naivedyam
Mangalore International (see Where to stay), KS Rao Rd.
Smart, superb value place for pure veg cooking, with a/c and non-a/c sections.

$ Surabhi
Opposite the KSRTC State Bus Stand, Lalbagh.
Tandoori and cold beer, handy if waiting for a night bus.

$ Taj Mahal
Hampankatta Circle.
Dingy ancient joint serving superb chilli-laden *upma*, crispy *dosa* and good cheap juices.

Shopping

Athree Book Centre, *Sharavasthi Bldg (below Quality Hotel), Balmatta Rd, T0824-242 5161.* Excellent selection of English-language novels and non-fiction.

What to do

Swimming
The swimming pool at **Moti Mahal hotel** (see Where to stay) is open to non-residents for Rs 120 per hr.

Tour operators
Trade Wings, *Lighthouse Hill Rd, Mangalore, T0824-242 6225.* A useful agent providing good service. Can change TCs and arrange flight bookings.

Transport

Air
Bajpe Airport is 22 km north of town and has connections with **Bengaluru**, **Hyderabad**, **Chennai**, **Mumbai**, **Delhi**, as well as several cities in the Gulf. A taxi

to/from town costs Rs 400; shared taxi Rs 100; **Indian Airlines** also runs an airport coach. **Indian Airlines**, Hathill Complex, Lalbag, T0824-245 1045, airport, T0824-225 4253. **Jet Airways**, Ram Bhavan Complex, Kodialbail, T0824-244 1181, airport, T0824-225 2709

Bus

Mangalore has 2 main bus stands for intercity buses: the convenient **Central** or **State Bank Bus Stand**, used by private companies; and the **KSRTC Bus Stand**, north of the centre, used by government buses.

KSRTC Long-Distance Bus Stand, Bajjai Rd, is 3 km north of the centre, T0824-2211243; to get to the town centre and railway, leave the bus station, turn left for 50 m to the private bus shelter and take bus Nos 19 or 33. The station is well organized; the booking hall at the entrance has a computer printout of the timetable in English. The main indicator board shows different bus categories: **red** – ordinary; **blue** – semi-deluxe; **green** – super-deluxe. (*Exp* buses may be reserved 7 days ahead). **Mysore** and **Bengaluru**: 296 km, 7 hrs and 405 km, 9 hrs, every 30 mins from 0600 (route via Madikeri is the best); trains take 20 hrs. **Chennai** 717 km; **Madurai** 691 km, 16 hrs. **Panaji**, 10 hrs.

Buses serve several destinations including **Bengaluru**, **Bijapur**, **Goa**, **Ernakulam**, **Hampi**, **Gokarna**, **Kochi**, **Mumbai** and **Udupi**.

Rickshaw

Minimum charge Rs 10, though arriving at the **Central** train station or bus stand at night you'll be charged extra. Rs 100 to **Kankanadi Station** from the centre.

Train

Mangalore has 2 train stations. Trains starting and finishing in Mangalore use the **Central Station**; trains on the Mumbai–Kerala line stop at the newer **Mangalore Junction** station at Kankanadi, 10 km east of the city.

From Central Station: **Bengaluru**, *Yesvantpur Exp 16518/16524*, 2055, 11½ hrs, via **Hassan** (6 hrs). **Chennai**: *Mangalore Mail 12602* (AC/II), 1315, 16 hrs; *West Coast Exp 16628*, 2200, 18 hrs. Both via **Kozhikode**, 4 hrs, and Palakkad, 8 hrs. **Gokarna Rd**: *Matsyagandha Exp 12620* 1435, 4 hrs; *Mangalore Madgaon Pass 56640*, 0630, 4 hrs. **Madgaon (Margao)**: *Matsyagandha Exp 12620*, 1435, 6 hrs (on to Thane and Lokmanya Tilak for Mumbai). **Thiruvananthapuram** (17 hrs) via Kochi (9 hrs) and **Kollam** (15 hrs): *Malabar Express 16630*, 1820; *Ernad Exp 16605*, 0720.

From Kankanadi Station (Mangalore Junction): **Mumbai** (Lokmanya Tilak) via Madgaon: *Nethravati Exp 16346*, 2330, 17½ hrs.

Karnataka's Sapphire Coast

empty beaches, mangrove-fringed estuaries and India's biggest waterfall

Udupi (Udipi) → *Phone code: 0820. Population: 113,000.*

One of Karnataka's most important pilgrimage sites, Udupi is the birthplace of the 12th-century saint Madhva, who set up eight sannyasi *maths* (monasteries) in the town. Almost as well known today as the home of a family of Kanarese Brahmins who have established a chain of coffee houses and hotels across South India, it is a pleasant town, rarely visited by foreigners.

ON THE ROAD

Vegetarian victuals

The name of Udupi is associated across South India with authentic Brahmin cooking, which means vegetarian food at its best. But what is authentic Udupi cuisine? Pamela Philipose, writing in the *Indian Express*, suggests that strictly it is food prepared for temple use by Shivali Brahmins at the Krishna temple. It is therefore not only wholly vegetarian, but it also never uses onions or garlic.

Pumpkins and gourds are the essential ingredients, while *sambar*, which must also contain ground coconut and coconut oil, is its base. The spicy pepper water, *rasam*, is compulsory, as are the ingredients jackfruit, heart-shaped colocasia leaves, raw green bananas, mango pickle, red chilli and salt. *Adyes* (dumplings), *ajadinas* (dry curries) and chutneys, including one made of the skin of the ridge gourd, are specialities. Favourite dishes are *kosambiri* with pickle, coconut chutney and *appalam*. At least two vegetables will be served, including runner beans, and rice. Sweets include *payasa* and *holige*.

According to one legend the statue of Krishna once turned to give a low caste devotee *darshan*. The **Sri Krishna Math**, on Car Street in the heart of the town, is set around a large tank, the *Madhva Sarovar*, into which devotees believe that the Ganga flows every 10 years. There are some attractive *math* buildings with colonnades and arches fronting the temple square, as well as huge wooden temple chariots. This Hindu temple, like many others, is of far greater religious than architectural importance, and receives a succession of highly placed political leaders. Visitors are 'blessed' by the temple elephant. In the biennial **Paraya Mahotsava**, on 17/18 January of even-numbered years, the temple management changes hands (the priest-in-charge heads each of the eight *maths* in turn). The **Seven-Day Festival**, 9-15 January, is marked by an extravagant opening ceremony complete with firecrackers, dancing elephants, brass band and eccentric re-enactments of mythical scenes, while towering wooden temple cars, illuminated by strip lights followed by noisy portable generators, totter around the square, pulled by dozens of pilgrims.

Sri Ananthasana Temple, where Madhva is believed to have dematerialized while teaching his followers, is in the centre of the temple square. The eight important *maths* are around Car Street: Sode, Puthige and Adamar (south); Pejawar and Palamar (west); Krishna and Shirur (north); and Kaniyur (east).

Around Udupi

Some 5 km inland from Udupi, **Manipal** is a university town famous throughout Karnataka as the centre of *Yakshagana* dance drama, which like *Kathakali* in Kerala is an all-night spectacle. **Rashtrakavi Govind Pai Museum** ⓘ *MGM College*, has a collection of sculpture, bronze, inscriptions and coins.

There are good beaches north and south of Udupi, so far with little in the way of accommodation or infrastructure. The closest is at **Malpe**, 5 km west of

Udupi, but it's none too appealing: the fishing village at one end of the beach and the fish market on the docks are very smelly, and the beach itself is used as a public toilet in places. If you are prepared for a walk or cycle ride you can reach a deserted sandy beach.

Across the bay is the island of **Darya Bahadurgarh** and 5 km to the southwest is tiny **St Mary's Isle**, which is composed of dramatic hexagonal basalt; Vasco da Gama landed here in 1498 and set up a cross. Boats leave Malpe for the island from 1030; the last one returns at 1700, Rs 70 return.

Bhatkal

One of the many bullock cart tracks that used to be the chief means of access over the Western Ghats started from **Bhatkal**, a stop on the Konkan Railway. Now only a small town with a mainly Muslim population, in the 16th century it was the main port of the *Vijayanagar* Empire. It also has two interesting small temples. From the north, the 17th-century Jain **Chandranatha Basti** with two buildings linked by a porch, is approached first. The use of stone tiling is a particularly striking reflection of local climatic conditions, and is a feature of the Hindu temple to its south, a 17th-century **Vijayanagar Temple** with typical animal carvings. In the old cemetery of the church is the **tomb of George Wye** (1637), possibly the oldest British memorial in India.

Gokarna → *Phone code: 08386.*

Shaivite pilgrims have long been drawn to Gokarna by its temples and the prospect of a holy dip in the Arabian Sea, but it's the latter half of the equation that lures backpackers. The long, broad expanses of beach stretching along the coast, of which the graceful double curve of **Om Beach** is the most famous, provide an appealing alternative hideaway to Goa, and the busy little town centre plays host to some fascinating cultural inversions: pilgrims wade in the surf in full *salwar kameez* while hippy castaways in bikinis sashay past the temple. And whilst the unspoiled beaches south of town remain the preserve of bodysurfers, *djembe* players and frisbee throwers, the recent rise in incidences of rape (by outsiders, the locals hasten to point out) should serve to remind that travellers would do well to respect local sensitivities.

Gokarna's name, meaning 'cow's ear', possibly comes from the legend in which Siva emerged from the ear of a cow – but also perhaps from the ear-shaped confluence of the two rivers here. Ganesh is believed to have tricked Ravana into putting down the famous Atmalinga on the spot now sanctified in the **Mahabalesvara Temple**. As Ravana was unable to lift the lingam up again, it is called *Mahabala* ('the strong one'). The **Tambraparni Teertha** stream is considered a particularly sacred spot for casting the ashes of the dead.

Beaches around Gokarna

Most travellers head for the beaches to the south. The path from town passing **Kudle Beach** (pronounced *Koodlee*) is easy enough to follow but quite rugged, especially south of **Om Beach** (about 3 km), and should not be attempted with a full backpack during the middle of the day. Stretches of the track are also quite isolated, and even during the day it's advisable for single women to walk with a companion, especially on weekends when large groups of Indian men descend on the beaches with bottles of rum. Both Om and Kudle beaches can get extremely busy in season, when the combination of too many people, a shortage of fresh water and poor hygiene can result in dirty beaches. **Half Moon Beach** and **Paradise Beach**, popular with long-stayers, can be reached by continuing to walk over the headlands and are another 2 km or so apart.

Jog Falls

Inland from Honnavar, just south of Gokarna, these falls, the highest in India, are not the untamed spectacle they once were, but still make a stunning sight if you visit at the end of the wet season; the best times are from late November to early January. Come any earlier and you'll be grappling with leeches and thick mist; any later, and the falls will be more a trickle than a roar, thanks to the 50-km-long **Hirebhasgar Reservoir**, which regulates the flow of the Sharavati River in order to generate hydroelectricity. The **Mysore Power Corporation** releases water to the falls every second Sunday from 1000 to 1800, but even on a low-flow day the scenery and the rugged walk to the base of the falls make a visit worthwhile.

There are four falls. The highest is the **Raja**, with a fall of 250 m and a pool below 40 m deep. Next is the **Roarer**, while a short distance to the south is the **Rocket**, which shoots great gouts of water into the air. Finally comes the

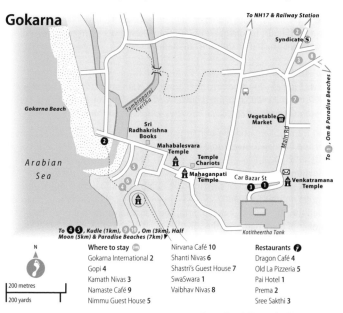

Gokarna

Where to stay		Nirvana Café **10**	Restaurants
Gokarna International **2**		Shanti Nivas **6**	Dragon Café **4**
Gopi **4**		Shastri's Guest House **7**	Old La Pizzeria **5**
Kamath Nivas **3**		SwaSwara **1**	Pai Hotel **1**
Namaste Café **9**		Vaibhav Nivas **8**	Prema **2**
Nimmu Guest House **5**			Sree Sakthi **3**

To **4 5**, Kudle (1km), **9 10**, Om (3km), Half
Moon (5km) & Paradise Beaches (7km)

200 metres
200 yards

Rani, which froths elegantly over rocks. A walk to the top (not possible in the monsoons) offers breathtaking views of the cascading river and the valley. Less ambitiously, you can get another excellent view from the Inspection Bungalow on the north side of the river gorge.

Project Seabird, Karwar and Anjedive

Karwar, on the banks of the Kalinadi River, is the administrative headquarters of North Kanara District. **Devbagh Beach**, off the coast, has a deep-water naval port protected by five islands. One of these was 'Anjedive' of old, known to seafarers centuries before Vasco da Gama called at the island in 1498, and the Portuguese built a fort there. It was later used as a Goan penal colony. From 1638 to 1752 there was an English settlement here, surviving on the pepper trade. The Portuguese held it for the next 50 years until the old town was destroyed in 1801. Today Karwar, strung out between the port and the estuary, has an unpleasant beach. However, the beaches a little to the south rival those of Goa but are still deserted. Also of interest are the hill fort, an octagonal church, and a 300-year-old temple.

India's Western Naval Command, which controls the 'sword arm' of the subcontinent's powerful Western fleet, has since the 1960s planned to move here from Mumbai – a principally commercial port and one that is worryingly close to Pakistani missiles – but work on the immense **Project Seabird** only began in October 1999. When complete it will become the largest naval base this side of the Suez Canal and will hold 140 plus warships, aircraft and repair dockyards, while the hillsides will be put to use concealing submarines. Karwar, crucially, is 900 nautical miles from Karachi versus Mumbai's 580. Since the area is under the control of the Navy it is off-limits to foreigners but driving past it gives a striking portrait of the subcontinent's military might and ambition.

Anshi-Dandeli Tiger Reserve

Enter via Dandeli, 110 km northeast of Karwar, or 74 km east of Hubli. Forest entry fees: Rs 1200, Indian Rs 400. Local forest guides rarely speak English, but staying at the Kali Adventure Camp or Old Magazine House will ensure access to a good naturalist.

Inland from Gokarna on the border with Goa, the conjoined national parks of Anshi and Dandeli protect more than 1000 sq km of endangered Western Ghats forests in the Kali River Basin, and rank as one of Karnataka's richest birding destinations. Some 200 species have been recorded, most notably the four species of hornbills – often seen in flocks numbering into the hundreds, with the rare great hornbill frequently spotted – as well as Sri Lankan frogmouth, orange-headed thrush and blue-headed pitta. The dense forests also provide habitat to a number of black panthers, though these, and the handful of tigers that call the park home, are very rarely seen. Whitewater rafting, jungle walks and jeep safaris are available around Dandeli town.

Where to stay

Udupi

$$-$ Srirama Residency
Opposite the post office, T0820-253 0761.
Top-quality new hotel with 30 excellent rooms, a bar, 2 restaurants and travel desk. Good service.

$$-$ Swadesh Heritage
MV Rd, T0820-252 9605,
www.hotelswadesh.com.
34 spotlessly clean rooms, 14 a/c, in this newish hotel (even the basic rooms are very good value) with 2 restaurants and a bar. Highly recommended.

$ Udupi Residency
Near the Service Bus Stand,
T0820-253 0005.
New hotel with 33 excellent rooms, 11 a/c, clean and well maintained. Restaurant on site. Highly recommended.

Around Udupi

$$ Valley View International
On campus, Manipal, T0820-257 1101.
Has 70 good a/c rooms with upmarket facilities including a pool. Recommended.

$ Green Park
Manipal, T0820-257 0562.
38 rooms, some of which are a/c.
Also has a restaurant.

$ Silver Sands
Thottam Beach, 1 km north of Malpe,
T0820-253 7223.
8 pleasant cottages and a restaurant with limited menu. Friendly; recommended.

$ Tourist Home
Halfway to Thotham Beach, Malpe.
4 pleasant, seaside rooms.

Gokarna

$ Kamath Nivas
Main Rd, T08386-256035.
Newish, simple rooms, some with TVs and balconies overlooking the road.

$ Nimmu Guest House
Near the temple, Mani Bhadra Rd, T08386-256730, nimmuhouse@yahoo.com.
Small but decent rooms spread across 2 separate wings; the 5 newest rooms are better value as they are big, bright and catch the breeze. There's also limited roof space for overspill, and a garden. The whole place is laid-back and friendly, and has safe luggage storage. Recommended.

$ Shanti Nivas
Gayatri Rd (behind Nimmu's), T08386-256983.
Set in a coconut grove just inland from the south end of Gokarna Beach. Choose from clean simple rooms in the main house, apartments in the annexe, or a couple of solid hexagonal huts with mosquito nets and mattresses.

$ Shastri's Guest House
Main Rd near the bus stand, T08386-256220.
24 rooms with bath, some have up to 4 beds. Set back from the road, it's a bit gritty but quiet and decent value. Luggage storage.

$ Vaibhav Nivas
Ganjigadde off Main Rd (5 mins' walk from the bazar), T08386-256714.
Family-run guesthouse with small rooms, and an annexe with 10 rooms, some with bath (Indian and Western WC). Meals and luggage storage available.

Beaches around Gokarna

The cafés along **Gokarna**, **Kudle**, **Om** and **Paradise** beaches let out mud and palm leaf huts with shared facilities (often just one squat toilet and a palm-screened shower) for Rs 50-150 a night during season; many are closed Apr-Oct. The more expensive huts come with thin mattresses, fans and mosquito nets, but little in the way of security. The guesthouses in town offer to store luggage for a small charge. The options listed below are secure.

$$$$ SwaSwara
Om Beach, 15 mins from town, T08386-257131, www.swaswara.com.
Elite retreat with 'yoga for the soul' on 12-ha complex on the curve of gorgeous Om Beach. Classes taught by Indian *swamis* include: ashtanga, hasya, kundalini, yoga nidra (psychic sleep) and meditation. From the hilltop the thatched Konkan stone villas look like an Ewok village, with private gardens and a pool; beds are strewn with flowers in the day and philosophical quotes in the evening. But despite its size and expense the resort has virtually no visual impact on the beach, and fishermen can still shelter under the mangroves out front. Also offers Ayurveda, archery, kayaking, trekking, butterfly and birdwatching, and jungle walks.

$ Gokarna International Resort
Kudle Beach, T08386-257843.
The smartest rooms on Kudle Beach, some with sea-facing balconies. Ayurvedic massages on site.

$ Namaste Café
Om Beach, T08386-257141. Open all year.
The hub of Om's traveller scene has adequate en suite rooms, some with beach views, and a cute but not mosquito-proof bamboo cottage up in the woods. Travel agent, internet and food available.

$ Nirvana Café
Om Beach, T08386-329851.
A pleasant complex under some coconut trees, with a choice of basic huts and solid concrete-and-tile cottages.

Jog Falls

Hotels are very basic and there are very limited eating facilities at night. Local families take in guests. Stalls near the falls serve reasonable breakfast and meals during the day.

$ Mayura Gerusoppa (KSTDC)
Sagar Taluk, T08186-244732.
This decaying concrete hotel overlooking the falls has 22 rooms and a 10-bed dorm.

$ PWD Inspection Bungalow
West of the falls, T08186-244333.
Just a handful of neat a/c rooms, preferable to the various KSTDC options, but a challenge to book.

$ Youth Hostel
Shimoga Rd, T08186-244251.
Utterly basic dorms with mattresses on the floor.

Anshi-Dandeli Tiger Reserve

$$$$ Kali Adventure Camp
Dandeli, T080-4055 4055, www.junglelodges.com.
Professionally run rafting and safari camp, with comfortable cottages, tents and overpriced dorms. The best rooms face right onto the river. Rates include daily jeep safaris and coracle rides on the Kali to spot crocodiles and birds; whitewater rafting costs extra.

$$ Old Magazine House
Ganeshgudi village, T080-4055 4055, www.junglelodges.com.

This small encampment of spartan but comfortable bamboo huts is dedicated to birdwatchers, with bird baths throughout the property attracting a huge range of semi-tame birds. Great for photographers.

Restaurants

Udupi

$ Dwarike
Car St, facing Temple Sq.
Immaculately clean, modern, good service, comfortable, Western and South Indian food, excellent snacks, ice creams.

$ Gokul
Opposite Swadesh Heritage (see Where to stay).
Excellent vegetarian, good value.

$ Mitra Samaj
Car St.
Full of pilgrims from the nearby Krishna temple, this humble place churns out endless plates of idli, vada and dozens of variety of dosa.

Gokarna

Cheap vegetarian *thalis* are available near the bus stand and along Main St while places towards the town beach serve up the usual array of pancakes, falafel, spaghetti and burgers. Standards are improving on the southern beaches, with Nepali-run kitchens dishing out traveller food, often of excellent quality. If you don't want to add to the mounds of plastic bottles littering the beaches, ask around for cafés that will let you fill your bottle from their cooler – it should cost a little less than the price of a new bottle.

$ Dragon Café
Kudle Beach.

Good *thalis* and *pakora*, excellent pizza and, perhaps, the best mashed potato in Gokarna.

$ Old La Pizzeria
Kudle.
Popular hangout joint. Laundry and internet facilities as well as good Western food.

$ Pai Hotel
Near Venkatramana Temple in Main St.
Good *masala dosa*.

$ Prema
By the car park at Gokarna Beach.
Serves great fruit salads, the best *gudbad* in town and its own delicious soft garlic cheese, but popularity has resulted in slow and surly service.

$ Sree Sakthi
Near Venkatramana Temple.
Superb ice cream and Indian food, comfort snacks (try the home-made oil-free peanut butter on toast). Basic but clean and well run.

Karwar

$$ Fish Restaurant
In the Sidvha Hotel.
Excellent bistro-type place.

Shopping

Gokarna
Sri Radhakrishna Books, *on main road near the beach*. Tiny bookshop with an astonishingly good range of beach reads.

What to do

Gokarna
You can hire canoes from a small office on the northern part of Om Beach for Rs 200 per hr.

Transport

Udupi
Bus
Udupi's **State** and **Private bus stands** are next to each other in the central square. From Udupi, frequent service to **Mangalore** (1½ hrs). Mornings and evenings to **Bengaluru** and **Mysore** from 0600; **Hubli** from 0900; **Dharmashala**, from 0600-0945, 1400-1830; **Mumbai** at 1120, 1520, 1700, 1920.

Train
The station is 5 km from the town centre; auto, Rs 90. All express and passenger trains between Mangalore and Madgaon in Goa stop here.

Gokarna
Boat
Boatmen on Om Beach quote Rs 300-500 for a dropoff to either **Gokarna** or **Paradise Beach**, or Rs 50-100 per person if there's a group. Return trips to Paradise Beach may only give you 30 mins on land.

Bus
KSRTC buses provide a good service: **Chaudi** 2 hrs; **Karwar** (via Ankola) frequent (1 hr); **Hospet** 1430 (10 hrs); **Margao**, 0815 (4 hrs); **Mangalore** via **Udupi** 0645 (7 hrs); **Panaji** 0800 (5 hrs). Private sleeper buses to **Bengaluru** and **Hampi** can be booked from agents in the bazar; most depart from Kumta or Ankola.

Taxi
Most hotels and lodges offer to organize taxis, but often quote excessive prices; no destination seems to be less than 100 km away. To **Gokarna Rd**, bargain for Rs 120; to **Ankola**, around Rs 550.

Train
Gokarna Road Station is 10 km from town, 2 km from the NH17; most trains are met by auto-rickshaws and minibus taxis: Rs 125 to Gokarna Bus Stand, Rs 200 to Om Beach. State buses to/from Kumta pass the end of the station road, a 1-km walk from the station. **Madgaon** (**Margao**): *Matsyagandha Exp 12620*, 1840, 2 hrs; *Mangalore-Madgaon Pass 56640*, 1023, 2¼ hrs. **Mangalore** (**Central**): *Madgaon-Mangalore Pass 56641*, 1528, 5 hrs.

Jog Falls
Bus
Daily buses connect Jog Falls with **Honnavar** (2½ hrs) and **Karwar**, both on the Konkan railway line; some Honnavar buses continue to **Kumta** (3 hrs), which has frequent services to **Gokarna**. Direct buses also go daily to **Mangalore** (7hrs), **Bengaluru** (9 hrs), and **Panaji**. Hourly buses to **Shimoga** (4 hrs) for connections to **Belur**, **Hassan** and **Hospet** (7 hrs from Shimoga). For a wider choice of departures get a local bus to **Sagar**. 30 km southeast on NH-206.

Taxi
To **Panaji**, Rs 1500 (6 hrs).

Train
Jog Falls is 16 km from the railway at **Talguppa**. Trains from **Bengaluru** (**Bangalore**) involve a change in **Shimoga** town.

Karwar
Bus
To **Jog Falls**, 0730 and 1500 (6 hrs). Frequent buses to **Palolem**, **Margao** (Madgaon) and **Panaji**, also direct buses to **Colva**. Buses often full; you may have to fight to get on. The road crosses the Kali River (car toll Rs 5) then reaches the Goa border and check post (8 km north).

Northern
Karnataka

ancient caves, temples and a famous 15th-century fort

Down the centuries, northeast Karnataka has been host to a profusion of Deccani rulers. Hampi, site of the capital city of the Vijayanagar Hindu Empire that rose to conquer the entire south in the 14th century, is the region's most famous, and is an extraordinary site of desolate temples, compounds, stables and pleasure baths, surrounded by a stunning boulder-strewn landscape. The cluster of temple relics in the villages of Aihole, Pattadakal and Badami dates from the sixth century, when the Chalukyans first started experimenting with what went on to become the distinct Indian temple design. Nearby are the Islamic relics of Bijapur and Bidar, sudden plots of calm tomb domes with their Persian inscriptions ghosted into lime, and archways into empty harems; all the more striking for being less visited.

Climb any boulder-toppled mountain around the ruins of the Vijayanagar Empire and you can see the dizzying scale of the Hindu conquerors' glory; Hampi was the capital of a kingdom that covered the whole of southern India. Little of the kingdom's riches remain; now the mud huts of gypsies squat under the boulders where noblemen once stood, while the double-decker shopfronts of the old Hampi Bazar, where diamonds were once traded by the kilo, have transformed into a more prosaic marketplace geared to profiting from Western tourists and domestic pilgrims. Yet away from the hubbub and hassle of the bazar – somewhat reduced since 2012 when the Archaeological Survey of India sent in bulldozers to knock down many of the 'unauthorized' houses and shops – Hampi possesses a romantic, hypnotic desolation that's without parallel in South India. You'll need at least a full day to get a flavour of the place, but for many visitors the chilled-out vibe has a magnetic attraction, and some end up staying for weeks.

Visiting Hampi
Buses and trains arrive in Hospet, from where it is a 30-minute rickshaw (around Rs 200) or bus ride to Hampi. The site is spread out, so hiring a bicycle is a good idea though some paths are too rough to ride on. You enter the area from the west at Hampi Bazar or from the south at Kamalapuram.

Sacred Centre
The road from the west comes over Hemakuta Hill, overlooking the Sacred Centre of **Vijayanagar** (the 'Town of Victory'), with the **Virupaksha Temple** and the Tungabhadra River to its north. On the hill are two large monolithic Ganesh sculptures and some small temples. The road runs down to the village and the once world-famous market place. You can now only see the wide pathway running east from the towering **Virupaksha Temple** (*Pampapati*) with its nine-storey *gopuram*, to where the bazar once hummed with activity. The temple is still in use; note the interesting paintings on the *mandapam* ceiling.

Riverside
You can walk along the river bank (1500 m) to the famous **Vitthala Temple**. The path is easy and passes several interesting ruins including small 'cave' temples – worthwhile with a guide. Alternatively, a road skirts the Royal Enclosure to the south and goes all the way to the Vitthala Temple. On the way back (especially if it's at sunset) it's worth stopping to see **Raghunatha Temple**, on a hilltop, with its Dravidian style, quiet atmosphere and excellent view of the countryside from the rocks above.

After passing **Achyuta Bazar**, which leads to the **Tiruvengalanatha Temple**, 400 m to the south, the riverside path goes near **Sugriva's Cave**, where it is said that Sita's jewels, dropped as she was abducted by the demon Ravana, were hidden by Sugriva. There are good views of the ancient ruined bridge to the east. Nearby the path continues past the only early period Vaishnavite shrine, the 14th-century **Narasimha Temple**. The **King's Balance** is at the end of the path as it approaches the Vitthala Temple. It is said that the rulers were weighed against gold, jewels and food, which were then distributed to Brahmins.

Vitthala Temple ⓘ *0830-1700, US$5/ Rs 250, allows entry to Lotus Mahal on the same day.* A World Heritage Monument, the Vitthala Temple is dedicated to Vishnu. It stands in a rectangular courtyard enclosed within high walls. Probably built in the mid-15th century, it is one of the oldest and most intricately carved temples, with its *gopurams* and *mandapas*. The *Dolotsava mandapa* has 56 superbly sculpted slender pillars which can be struck to produce different musical notes. It has elephants on the balustrades and horses at the entrance. The other two ceremonial *mandapas*, though less finely carved, nonetheless depict some interesting scenes, such as Krishna hiding in a tree from the *gopis* and a woman using a serpent twisted around a stick to churn a pot of buttermilk. In the courtyard is a superb chariot carved out of granite, the wheels raised off the ground so that they could be revolved!

Krishnapura
On the road between the Virupaksha Bazar and the Citadel you pass Krishnapura, Hampi's earliest Vaishnava township with a Chariot Street 50 m wide and 600 m long, which is now a cultivated field. **Krishna Temple** has a very impressive gateway to the east. Just southwest of the Krishna temple is the colossal monolithic **statue of Lakshmi**

Essential Northern Karnataka

Finding your feet

The closest airport to Hampi is at Hubli (Hubballi), three hours' drive to the west, with flights from Bengaluru, Chennai and Mumbai. Hospet is the area's main transport hub with regular long-distance buses from major towns and cities. It is a 30-minute rickshaw ride to both entrances at Hampi. The Kamalapuram road is better, especially in the rainy season when the slower road to Hampi Bazar is barely passable. Badami is the best base for visiting the Cradle of Hindu architecture temples at Pattadakal, Aihole and Mahakuta, though hiring a car and driver is the most comfortable option. The nearest train station for visiting Hampi is at Hospet, which has regular connections with most major towns. Bijapur, Badami, Gulbarga and Bidar all have train stations with good connections.

When to go

The high season is November to January but accommodation prices can rise by up to 30% during this time. Rooms in Hampi are packed out during the music festival in early November. During the rainy season the road from Hospet to Hampi Bazar is barely passable.

Time required

At least a day to visit Hampi, though you could easily spend several days or weeks here soaking up the atmosphere. The Cradle of Hindu architecture temples can be seen in a day though this might be a push if using public transport.

Narasimha in the form of a four-armed man-lion with fearsome bulging eyes sheltered under a seven-headed serpent, Ananta. It is over 6 m high but sadly damaged.

The road south, from the Sacred Centre towards the Royal Enclosure, passes the excavated **Prasanna Virupaksha Temple** (misleadingly named 'underground') and interesting watchtowers.

Hampi-Vijayanagar

Royal Enclosure

At the heart of the metropolis is the small **Hazara Rama Temple**, the Vaishanava 'chapel royal'. The outer enclosure wall to the north has five rows of carved friezes while the outer walls of the *mandapa* has three. The episodes from the epic *Ramayana* are told in great detail, starting with the bottom row of the north end of the west *mandapa* wall. The two-storey **Lotus Mahal** ⓘ *0600-1800, US$5/Rs250, allows entry to Vitthala Temple on the same day*, is in the **Zenana** or ladies' quarter, screened off by its high walls. The watchtower is in ruins but you can see the domed **stables** for 10 elephants with a pavilion in the centre and the guardhouse. Each stable had a wooden beamed ceiling from which chains were attached to the elephants' backs and necks. In the **Durbar Enclosure** is the specially built decorated platform of the **Mahanavami Dibba**, from which the royal family watched the pageants and tournaments during the nine nights of *navaratri* festivities. The 8-m-high square platform originally had a covering of bricks, timber and metal but what remains still shows superb carvings of hunting and battle scenes, as well as dancers and musicians.

The exceptional skill of water engineering is displayed in the excavated system of aqueducts, tanks, sluices and canals, which could function today. The attractive **Pushkarini** is the 22-sq-m stepped tank at the centre of the enclosure. The road towards Kamalapuram passes the **Queen's Bath**, in the open air, surrounded by a narrow moat, where scented water filled the bath from lotus-shaped fountains. It measures about 15 m by 2 m and has interesting stucco work around it.

Daroji Bear Sanctuary
15 km from Hampi Bazar, daily 0600-1800. Rs 1000, Indians Rs 200.

The relatively new Daroji sanctuary protects 55 sq km of boulder-strewn scrubland, which is home to around 120 sloth bears. The bears have become accustomed to regular treats of honey, courtesy of the park rangers, and a handful of them come regularly to a particular rock to feed. A watchtower placed high above the spot makes this perhaps the best place in India to observe the species in the wild. The sanctuary also has leopard, wolf, jackal, Eurasian horned owl, and good populations of the beautiful painted sandgrouse.

Hospet (Hosapete) → *Phone code: 08394. Population: 206,200.*
The transport hub for Hampi, Hospet is famous for its sugar cane; the town exports sugar across India, villagers boil the milk to make *jaggery* and a frothing freshly wrung cup costs you just Rs 4. Other industries include iron ore, biscuit making and the brewing of Royal Standard rum. The main bazar, with its characterful old houses, is interesting to walk around.

Tungabhadra Dam ⓘ *6 km west, Rs 5, local bus takes 15 mins,* is 49 m high and offers panoramic views. One of the largest masonry dams in the country, it was completed in 1953 to provide electricity for irrigation in the surrounding districts.

Muharram, the Muslim festival that marks the death of Mohammed's grandson Imam Hussein, is celebrated with a violent vigour both here and in the surrounding

BACKGROUND

Hampi

Hampi was founded on the banks of the Tungabhadra River in 1336 by two brothers, Harihara and Bukka, and rose to become the seat of the mighty Vijayanagar Empire and a major centre of Hindu rule and civilization for 200 years. The city, which held a monopoly on the trade of spices and cotton, was enormously wealthy – some say greater than Rome – and the now-sorry bazar was packed with diamonds and pearls, the crumbled palaces plated with gold. Although it was well fortified and defended by a large army, the city fell to a coalition of northern Muslim rulers, the Deccan Sultans, at Talikota in 1565. The invading armies didn't crave the city for themselves, and instead sacked it, smiting symbolic blows to Hindu deities and taking huge chunks out of many of the remaining white granite carvings. Today, the craggy 26-sq-km site holds the ghost of a capital complete with aqueducts, elephant stables and baths as big as palaces. The dry arable land is slowly being peeled back by archaeologists to expose more and more of the kingdom's ruins.

The site for the capital was chosen for strategic reasons, but the craftsmen adopted an ingenious style to blend in their architectural masterpieces with the barren and rocky landscape. Most of the site is early 16th century, built during the 20-year reign of Krishna Deva Raya (1509-1529) with the citadel standing on the bank of the river.

villages and with equal enthusiasm by both the area's significant Muslim population and Hindus. Ten days of fasting is broken with fierce drum pounding, drink and frequent arguments, sometimes accompanied by physical violence. Each village clusters around icons of Hussein, whose decapitation is represented by a golden crown on top of a face covered with long strings of jasmine flowers held aloft on wooden sticks. Come evening, fires are lit. When the embers are dying villagers race through the ashes, a custom that may predate Islam's arrival. The beginnings or ends of livestock migrations to seasonal feeding grounds are marked with huge bonfires. Cattle are driven through the fires to protect them from disease. Some archaeologists suggest that Neolithic ash mounds around Hospet were the result of similar celebrations over 5000 years ago.

Tourist information

Tourist office
On the approach to Virupaksha Temple,
Hampi-Vijayanagar, T08394-241339.
Open 0800-1230, 1500-1830.
A 4-hr guided tour of the site (without
going into the few temples that charge
admission) costs around Rs 250.

Where to stay

Some use Hospet as a base for
visiting Hampi; it has plusher
accommodation and the nearest
railway station. However, it means a
30-min commute to Hampi. Hampi
is quieter, more basic and infinitely
more atmospheric – though note
that the ASI still has notional plans to
bulldoze the entire village of Hampi
Bazar, so ring in advance. Across the
river (by *coracle* or ferry, Rs 15) you can
reach the hamlet of Virupapur Gaddi,
a beautiful paddy-planted village
with budget guesthouses, coco-huts
and cottages to stay in. Power cuts
are common both sides of the river –
a supply of candles and a torch are
essential – and mosquitoes can be a
real menace. A small selection of the
many guesthouses are listed here. All
are similar and mostly in the **$** price
category; prices rise 30% at the height
of the season, Nov-Jan.

$$$$ Sloth Bear Resort
Near Kannada University, Kamalapur,
bookings T080-4055 4055, www.
junglelodges.com.
Excellent new nature resort, with tribal-
style stone-and-thatch cottages set amid
scrub a 20-min drive from Hampi Bazar.

Good birding safaris, visits to Daroji
Bear Sanctuary and a sunrise trip to
Hampi are included. Good food and
attentive service.

$$$-$ Mayura Bhuvaneswari
2 km from the site, Kamalapuram,
T08394-241574.
Government-run place that feels both
weird and worn out; the budget rooms
are overpriced, grimy and falling apart,
while the newer suites have bizarre
ultraviolet tube lights that lend the feel
of sleeping in an abandoned nightclub.
Decent food and chilled beer, but service
is stretched.

$ Archana
Janata Plot, T08394-241547,
addihampi@yahoo.com.
The pick of the Hampi Bazar hotels,
with 9 clean, quiet rooms (some a/c),
good atmosphere and great views
from the roof.

$ Gopi
Janata Plot (in the lane behind
Shanti Guest House), T08394-241695,
kirangopi2002@yahoo.com.
Clean rooms with hot water, those
in the older wing have Indian toilets.

$ Mowgli Guest House
1.5 km from the ferry in Virupapur
Gaddi, T08533-287033,
www.mowglihampi.com.
A wide selection of rooms, from basic
cells with shared bath to cute circular
huts and lovely bright a/c rooms on the
2nd floor with expansive views over
stunningly green paddy fields terracing
down to the river. Hot water a few hours
a day, international restaurant and pool
table. Mellow without being too mellow.

$ Padma Guest House
T08394-241331.
Family guesthouse with 4 double rooms and currency exchange.

$ Rahul
South of the bus stand.
Quite quiet despite being near the bus stand. Basic but clean accommodation under nets. Good simple vegetarian food and views from the rooftop.

$ Ranjana Guest House
Behind Govt school, T08394-241330.
A friendly guesthouse with 5 rooms, plus hot water, cheaper rooms have a cooler, rather than a/c.

$ Shambhu
Janata Plot, T08394-241383, rameshhampi@yahoo.com.
5 rooms with bath and nets, plenty of plants. Rooftop restaurants (several egg dishes). Friendly.

$ Shanthi Guest House
Next to Mowgli, Virupapur Gaddi, T08394-325352, shanthi.hampi@ gmail.com.
More chilled-out than its neighbour, with atmospheric mud huts and a lovely covered lounge gazing out over the swaying rice and watching the sunset. Good service, hot water by the bucket.

$ Vicky
200 m north of the main road (turn off at the tourist office), T08394-241694, vickyhampi@yahoo.co.in.
7 rooms (4 with bath) with bucket hot water and Indian toilets, but there's a good rooftop restaurant and internet.

Hospet
Station Rd has been renamed Mahatma Gandhi Rd (MG Rd).

$$$$-$$$ Malligi
6/143 Jambunatha Rd, T08394-228101, www.malligihotels.com.
188 a/c rooms and large suites. Facilities include a restaurant, bar by the pool (non-residents pay Rs 25 per hr), health club, exchange, travel agent (good Hampi tour). The internet is creakingly slow and the STD/ISD service overpriced, but it's generally a pleasant place.

$$-$ Karthik
252 Sardar Patel Rd, T08394-220038.
40 good-sized clean rooms (10 a/c) in a quiet modern hotel with garden dining. Friendly and good value.

$$-$ Shanbhag Towers
College Rd, T08394-225910, shanbhagtowers@yahoo.com.
64 spacious rooms, 32 a/c with tub, TV, fridge, in this brand new hotel with a breathtaking Hampi theme. There are restaurants (one rooftop with great views) and a bar.

$ Nagarjuna Residency
Sardar Patel Rd, opposite Karthik, T08394-229009.
Spotless, modern, excellent value rooms, some a/c, extra bed Rs 30-50, very helpful. Recommended.

$ The Shine
Near the bus stand, Station Rd, T08394-694233, www.sainakshatra.com.
Sparkly new business hotel, with functional but pleasant and clean rooms, hot water and lift. Excellent value.

$ Shivananda
Next to the bus stand, T08394-220700.
23 rooms, 4 a/c, simple but clean, and complete with resident astrologer.

$ SLV Yatri Nivas
Station Rd, T08394-221525.
15 bright, airy rooms and dormitory in a clean, well-run hotel. Good vegetarian restaurant and bar.

$ Viswa
MG Rd, opposite the bus station, away from the road, T08394-227171.
42 basic rooms (some 4-bed) with bath, adjacent **Shanthi** restaurant. No frills but good value.

Restaurants

All restaurants are vegetarian, eggs are sometimes available.

$ Boomshankar
On the path to the Vittahla Temple.
Well-prepared, fresh river fish.

$ Gopi
See Where to stay.
Good cheap *thalis*.

$ Mango Tree
Janata Plot.
One of the most famous names in town, with a multicultural menu, though its new location lacks the magic that made it a backpacker favourite.

$ Mayura Bhuvaneswari
Kamalapuram.
Cheap adequate meals.

$ New Shanti
Opposite Shanti Guest House, between Virupaksha Temple and the river.
Good carrot/apple/banana/chocolate cakes to order.

$ Suresh
30 m from New Shanti on the path towards the river.
Run by a very friendly family, made to order so takes a while, but worth the wait.

Hospet
The hotels serve chilled beer.

$$ Waves
Malligi.
The multi-cuisine restaurant is next to the pool and serves good food. There's also a bar.

$ Iceland
Station Rd, behind the bus station.
Good South Indian meals.

$ Shanbhag
Near the bus station.
Good South Indian cuisine.

Festivals

Jan-Feb Virupaksha Temple Car festival.
3-5 Nov Hampi Music festival at Vitthala Temple when hotels get packed.

What to do

Hospet
Tour operators
Tours from KSTDC, T08394-221008; **KSRTC**, T08394-228537; and **SRK Tours and Travels** at Malligi Hotel, T08394-224188. All run day-tours to Hampi, some also including Tungabhadra Dam; Rs 100-150 per person. Day trips also go to Aihole, Badami and Pattadakal, 0830-1930, Rs 350 per person, but it's a very long day. Local sightseeing by taxi Rs 800 per day. Bijapur 1-day trip by bus Rs 175, taxi Rs 2100. English-speaking guide but rather rushed.

Transport

Air
The closest airport to Hampi is at Hubli (Hubballi), 3 hrs' drive to the west, with

flights from Bengaluru, Chennai and Mumbai.

Bicycle hire
Any guesthouse in Hampi Bazar can help you organize bike or scooter hire (bikes Rs 30-40 per day; scooters Rs 200 plus fuel).

Bus
Buses to/from Hospet run every 30 mins from the bazar. A few KSRTC long-distance buses also go to **Bengaluru** and **Goa**. Agents in the bazar sell train tickets and seats on overnight sleeper buses to Goa and **Gokarna**, most of which leave from Hospet.

Coracles and ferries
Boats take passengers across the river from the jetty west of the Virupaksha Temple, Rs 5 (Rs 10 with luggage). Services stop early in the evening; check the time of the last boat to avoid getting stranded.

Hospet
Bus
Frequent buses to **Hampi**'s 2 entry points (Kamalapuram and Hampi Bazar, both taking around 30 mins), from 0530; last return around 2000. The Kamalapuram road is better, especially in the rainy season when the slower road to Hampi Bazar is barely passable.

From the busy bus stand, T08394-228802, express buses run to/from **Bengaluru** (10 hrs) and **Mysore**

(10½ hrs). Several daily services to other sites, eg **Badami** (6 hrs), **Bijapur** (6 hrs), **Chitradurga** (3 hrs). More comfortable **Karnataka Tourism** luxury coaches run overnight to various towns. A few buses go direct to **Panaji** (**Goa**) – *Luxury*, 0630 (10½ hrs), State bus, 0830 (reserve a seat in advance); others involve a change in **Hubli** (4½ hrs). **Paulo Travels Luxury Sleeper** coach from Hotel Priyadarshini, at 1845, Rs 350, daily; **West Coast Sleeper**, from Hotel Shanbhag, 1830, Rs 350; daily (Oct-Mar only); strangers are expected to share a bunk. It's better to take a train to **Londa** (under 5 hrs) and get a bus to **Madgaon** or **Panaji** (3 hrs).

Rickshaw
From the train station to the bus stand should cost about Rs 30. To **Hampi**, Rs 150-200.

Taxi
KSTDC, T08394-21008, T08394-28537 or from Malligi Hotel; about Rs 700 per day.

Train
Bengaluru, *Hampi Exp 16591*, 2045 (via Guntakal, 2½ hrs) 10½ hrs. For **Belur/Halebid**: *Amaravati Exp 17225*, 0635 to **Hubli**; then *Hubli-Arsikere Pass 56274* (**S**), 1530. To **Badami**: via **Gadag**, 4 hrs. **Hyderabad (via Guntakal)**: *Amaravati Exp 17226*, 1450, 14 hrs. **Madgaon**, *Amaravati Exp 18047*, Mon, Wed, Thu, Sat 0630, 7 hrs. From nearby **Gadag**, train to **Bijapur**: *Hubli-Solapur Exp 11424*, 1620, 4½ hrs.

Bijapur (Vijayapura) → Phone code: 08352. Population: 326,400.

fascinating Islamic city of mosques, mausoleums, palaces and forts

Mohammed Adil Shah was not a man to be ignored; the tomb he built from the first day of his rule in anticipation of his own death hovers with dark magnificence over Bijapur and is so large it can be seen from over 20 km away. His brooding macabre legacy threw down the gauntlet to his immediate successor. Ali Adil Shah II, who took over from Mohammed in 1656, began his own tomb, which would surely have been double in size and architectural wonder had he not died too soon, 26 years into his reign, with only archways complete. His Bara Kamaan is nearby, while to the north of the city lies Begum's equally thwarted attempt to match Mohammed's strength in death. With its mausoleums, palaces and some of the finest mosques in the Deccan, Bijapur has the air of a northern Muslim city and retains real character. The *chowk* between the bus station and MG Road is quite atmospheric in the evening.

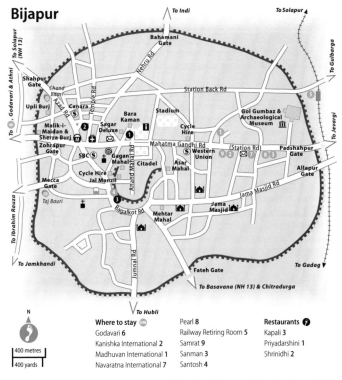

Where to stay
Godavari 6
Kanishka International 2
Madhuvan International 1
Navaratna International 7
Pearl 8
Railway Retiring Room 5
Samrat 9
Sanman 3
Santosh 4

Restaurants
Kapali 3
Priyadarshini 1
Shrinidhi 2

BACKGROUND

Bijapur

The Chalukyas who ruled over Bijapur were overthrown in the late 12th century. In the early years of the 14th century the Delhi Sultans took it for a time until the Bahmanis, with their capital in Gulbarga, ruled through a governor in Bijapur who declared Independence in 1489 and founded the Adil Shahi Dynasty. Of Turkish origin, they held power until 1686.

The 55-ton cannon was employed against Vijayanagar. Ali Adil Shah I, whose war it was, was somewhat chastened at the destruction his marauding Muslim armies had wreaked on the Hindu empire at Hampi. By way of atonement, and in a show of the inordinate riches that had fallen into his lap by supplanting Vijayanagar, he did his communal civic duty and built the exquisite Jama Masjid. It was his nephew Mohammed, he of the giant Gol Gumbaz, who later commissioned the Quaranic calligraphy that so sumptuously gilds the western wall.

Sights

The railway station is just outside the east wall of the fort less than 1 km from the Gol Gumbaz. Long-distance buses draw in just west of the citadel. Both arrival points are close enough to several hotels. It is easy to walk or cycle round the town. There are also autos and *tongas*; negotiate for the 'eight-sight tour price'.

Gol Gumbaz ⓘ *0630-1730, foreigners Rs 100, Indians Rs 5, video camera Rs 25, some choose to just view it from the gate.* Hulking in the background wherever you look in Bijapur is the vast whitewashed tomb of Mohammad Adil Shah, buried here with his wife, daughter and favourite court dancer, underneath the world's second largest dome (unsupported by pillars) – and one of its least attractive. Its extraordinary whispering gallery carries a message across 38 m which is repeated 11 times. However, noisy crowds make hearing a whisper quite impossible; it's quietest in the early morning. Numerous narrow steps in one of the corner towers lead to the 3-m-wide gallery. The plaster here was made out of eggs, cow dung, grass and jaggery. There is an excellent view of the city from the base of the dome. The **Nakkar Khana**, or gatehouse, is now a **museum** ⓘ *1000-1700, Rs 2*, housing an excellent collection of Chinese porcelain, parchments, paintings, armoury, miniatures, stone sculpture and old Bijapur carpets.

Jama Masjid To the south of Gol Gumbaz, this is one of the finest mosques in the Deccan, with a large shallow, onion-shaped dome and arcaded court. Built by Ali Adil Shah I (ruled 1557-1579) during Bijapur's rise to power it displays a classic restraint. The Emperor Aurangzeb added a grand entrance to the mosque and also had a square painted for each of the 2250 worshippers that it can accommodate.

West of here is the **Mehtar Mahal** (1620), whose delicate minarets and carved stone trellises were supposedly built for the palace sweepers.

Citadel Bijapur's Citadel, encircled by its own wall, now has few of its grand buildings intact. One is the Durbar Hall on the ground floor of **Gagan Mahal** ('Sky Palace'), open to the north so that the citizens outside were not excluded. It had royal residential quarters on either side with screened balconies for the women to remain unseen while they watched the court below. Another worth visiting is the **Jal Manzil**, or the water pavilion, a cool sanctuary. Just to the east is the **Asar Mahal** (circa 1646), once used as a court house with teak pillars and interesting frescoes in the upper floor.

Bara Kaman The Bara Kaman was possibly a 17th-century construction by Adil Shah III. Planned as a huge 12-storey building with the shadow of the uppermost storey designed to fall onto the tomb of the Gol Gumbaz, construction was ended after two storeys with the death of the ruler. An impressive series of arches on a raised platform is all that remains.

Sherza Burj The western gateway to the walled city, Sherza Burj (Lion Gate), has the enormous 55-tonne, 4.3-m-long, 1.5-m-diameter cannon **Malik-i-Maidan** (Ruler of the Plains). Cast in the mid-16th century in Ahmadnagar, it was brought back as a prize of war pulled by "400 bullocks, 10 elephants and hundreds of soldiers". The muzzle, a lion's head with open jaws, has an elephant being crushed to death inside, and the gun's roar was said to be so loud that the gunner used to dive into the tank off the platform to avoid being deafened. Inside the city wall nearby is **Upli Burj**, a 24-m-high watchtower with long guns and water tanks.

Ibrahim Rauza ⓘ *west of the city centre, 0600-1800, Rs 100, Indians Rs 5, video camera Rs 25, visit early morning to avoid crowds.* This palatial 17th-century tomb and mosque was built by Ibrahim Adil Shah during the dynasty's most prosperous period (after the sacking of Vijayanagar) when the arts and culture flourished. The corners of both buildings are decorated with slender minarets and decorative panels carved with lotus, wheel and cross patterns as well as bold Arabic calligraphy, bearing witness to the tolerance of the Adil Shahi Dynasty towards other religions. Near the Rauza is a huge tank, the **Taj Bauri**, built by Ibrahim II in memory of his wife. The approach is through a giant gateway flanked by two octagonal towers.

Listings Bijapur *map p89*

Tourist information

Tourist office
Opposite the stadium, Bijapur, T08352-250359. Mon-Sat 1030-1330 and 1415-1730. Not very useful.

Where to stay

There has been a sudden spurt in decent hotels and restaurants.

$$ Madhuvan International
Off Station Rd, T08352-255571.

35 rooms, 10 a/c, very pleasant, good vegetarian garden restaurant and rooftop terrace, beer in rooms only, travel desk, but a bit overpriced. Quite noisy till 2330 because of the restaurant.

$$-$ Hotel Kanishka International
Station Rd, T08352-223788, kanishka_bjp@rediffmail.com.
24 rooms en suite (10 a/c) with decidedly garish decor such as giant mirrors. Facilities include cable TV, telephone, laundry and the excellent **Kamat Restaurant** downstairs.

$ Godavari
Athni Rd, T08352-270828.
48 good rooms, friendly staff, good vegetarian and non-vegetarian food served.

$ Hotel Navaratna International
Station Rd, T08352-222771.
The grand colonnaded drive belies the modest price tag of the 34 rooms here (12 a/c). Communal areas scream with huge modernist paintings and rooms are done up with colour-coded care. TV, phone and smaller rooms have sit-outs. Very popular non-vegetarian courtyard restaurant, bar and pure vegetarian restaurant. They also have rooms and baths for drivers – a giant leap in the humane direction for an Indian hotel.

$ Hotel Pearl
Opposite Gol Gumbaz, Station Rd, T08352-256002.
32 rooms (17 a/c) in a modern, 3-storey, scrupulously clean, modest, mint pastel-coloured hotel set round a central courtyard with vegetarian basement restaurant (booze and non-vegetarian food through room service). Telephones, cable TV in all rooms, laundry and parking.

$ Railway Retiring Rooms
Also has a dorm. Very clean; contact the ticket collector on duty.

$ Samrat
Station Rd, T08352-250512.
30 basic rooms, 6 with a/c are passable, but the rest are battered. Good vegetarian garden restaurant but beware of the mosquitoes.

$ Sanman
Opposite Gol Gumbaz, Station Rd, T08352-251866.
24 clean (6 a/c), pleasant rooms with shower and mosquito nets. Very good value. Separate vegetarian and non-vegetarian restaurants with bar. Recommended.

$ Santosh
T08352-252179.
70 good, clean rooms including some a/c, quieter at the back, convenient, good value.

Restaurants

Most good places to eat are north of Sation Rd.

$ Kapali
Opposite bus stand.
Decent South Indian food.

$ Priyadarshini
MG Rd, opposite Gagan Mahal.
Vegetarian snacks.

$ Shrinidhi
Gandhi Chowk.
Quality vegetarian meals.

Festivals

Jan Siddhesvara Temple festival. Music festival accompanied by Craft Mela.

Transport

Bus

A service runs between the station and the west end of town. Horse-drawn carriages ply up and down MG Rd; bargain hard.

From the bus stand, T08352-251344, there are frequent services to **Bidar**, **Hubli**, **Belgaum** and **Solapur** (2-2½ hrs). Buses to **Badami**, 3½ hrs. For **Hospet**, travel via Gadag or Ikal. Reservations can be made on the following daily services to **Aurangabad**: 0600, 1830, **Hospet**, **Bengaluru**: 1700, 1800, 1930, 2130 (12 hrs), ultra-fast service at 1900, 2000; **Belgaum**: 0630, **Hubli**: 0900, 1400, 1600, **Hyderabad**: 0600, 1800, deluxe at 2130, **Mumbai (CT)**: 0800, 1600, 1700, 2030, **Mumbai (Kurla)**: 1900, 2000, 2100, **Mysore**: 1700, **Panaji**: 1900, and **Vasco de Gama**: 0715. Several private agents also run services to **Bengaluru**, **Mangalore**, **Mumbai** and **Pune** (7 hrs).

Train

Computerized Reservation Office opens 0800-2000, Sun 0800-1400. **Solapur**: 0945, 1635 (2½ hrs). **Gadag**: 5 trains daily for long-distance connections. Buses more convenient.

Cradle of Hindu temple architecture

Karnataka's best and most ancient temple architecture

Although Bijapur became an important Muslim regional capital, its surrounding region has several villages which, nearly 1500 years ago, were centres of Chalukyan power and the heart of new traditions in Indian temple building. At a major Indian crossroads, the temples at Aihole represent the first finely worked experiments in what were to become distinct North and South Indian temple styles.

Visiting the temples

Trains from Bijapur to Gadag stop at Badami, which makes a useful hub for visiting other sights. Buses run from Hubli, Hospet and Kolhapur. If you're travelling by bus it's best to visit Badami first, then Pattadakal and Aihole, but since it takes half a day to see Badami, visiting the sites by bus doesn't allow time for Mahakuta. If you want to see all the sights comfortably in a day it is well worth hiring a car in Bijapur, going to Aihole first and ending at Badami.

Aihole → Phone code: 0831.

The main temples are now enclosed in a park, open sunrise to sunset, foreigners Rs 100, Indians Rs 5, flash photography prohibited.

Aihole was the first Chalukyan capital, but the site was developed over a period of more than 600 years from the sixth century AD and includes important Rashtrakuta and late Chalukyan temples, some dedicated to Jain divinities. It is regarded as the birthplace of Indian temple architectural styles and the site of the first built temples, as distinct from those carved out of solid rock. Most of the temples were dedicated to Vishnu, though a number were subsequently converted into Shaivite shrines.

There are about 140 temples – half within the fort walls – illustrating a range of developing styles from Hoysala, Dravida, Jain, Buddhist, Nagara and Rekhanagara. There is little else. All the roads entering Aihole pass numerous temple ruins, but the road into the village from Pattadakal and Bagalkot passes the most important group of temples which would be the normal starting point for a visit. Some prefer to wander around the dozens of deserted (free) temples around town instead of joining the crowds in the park.

Durgigudi Temple Named not after the Goddess Durga but because it is close to the *durga* (fort), Durgigudi Temple dates from the late seventh century. It has an early *gopuram* structure and semi-circular apse which imitates early Buddhist *chaitya* halls. There are numerous superb sculptures including a series contained in niches around the ambulatory: walking clockwise they represent Siva and Nandi, Narasimha, Vishnu with Garuda, Varaha, Durga and Harihara.

Lad Khan Temple According to recent research Lad Khan Temple has been dated from around AD 700, not from AD 450 as suggested by the first Archaeological Survey of India reports in 1907. This is indicated by the similarity of some of its sculptures to those of the Jambulinga Temple at Badami, which has been dated precisely at AD 699. Originally an assembly hall and *kalyana mandapa* (marriage hall), it was named after Lad Khan, a pious Muslim who stayed in the temple at the end of the 19th century. A stone ladder through the roof leads to a shrine with damaged images of Surya, Vishnu and Siva carved on its walls. It bears a striking resemblance to the megalithic caves that were still being excavated in this part of the Deccan at the beginning of the period. The roof gives an excellent view of the village.

Gaudar Gudi Temple Close to the Lad Khan Temple, Gaudar Gudi is a small, rectangular Hindu temple, probably dating from the seventh century. It has a rectangular columned *mandapa*, surrounded on three sides by a corridor for circumambulation. Its roof of stone slabs is an excellent example of North Indian architecture.

Chikki Temple Beyond the Gaudar Gudi Temple is a small temple decorated with a frieze of pots, followed by a deep well. There are others in various states of repair. To see the most important of the remaining temples you leave the main park. Excavations are in progress, and the boundaries of the park may sometimes be fenced. Turning right out of the main park, the Bagalkot road leads to the Chikki Temple. Similar in plan to the Gaudar Gudi, this temple has particularly fine carved pillars. The beams which support the platform are also well worth seeing.

Ravan Phadi Cave Temple ⓘ *Reached from the main park entrance on the left, about 300 m from the village.* The cave itself (formerly known as the Brahman) is artificial, and the sixth-century temple has a variety of carvings of Siva both outside and inside. One is in the *Ardhanarisvara* form (half Siva, half Parvati), another depicts Parvati and Ganesh dancing. There is a huge lotus carved in the centre of the hall platform; and two small eighth-century temples at the entrance, the one to the northwest dedicated to Vishnu and that to the south, badly weathered, may have been based on an older Dravidian-style temple.

Buddhist Temple This is a plain two-storey temple on a hill beyond the end of the village on the way to the Meguti Temple. It has a serene smiling Buddha with the Bodhi Tree emerging from his head, on the ceiling of the upper floor. Further uphill is the **Jain temple**, a plain structure lacking the decorations on the plinth, columns and *gopuram* of many Hindu temples. It has a statue of Mahavira in the shrine within. Climb up through the roof for a good view of Aihole.

Meguti Temple Dating to AD 634, the Meguti Temple is reached from the Buddhist Temple down a path leading to a terrace. A left-hand route takes you to the foot of some stairs leading to the top of a hill which overlooks the town. This is the site of what is almost certainly the oldest building in Aihole and one of the oldest dated temples in India. Its date is indicated by an inscription by the court poet to the king Ravikirtti. A Dravidian-style temple, it is richly decorated on the outside, and although it has elements which suggest Shaivite origins, it has an extremely impressive seated Jain figure, possibly Neminath, in the sanctuary which comprises a hall of 16 pillars.

Kunti Group The Kunti Group is a group of four Hindu temples (dating from seventh to ninth centuries). To find them you have to return down to the village. The oldest is in the southeast. The external columns of its *mandapa* are decorated with *mithuna*, or erotic couples. The temple to the northwest has beautifully carved ceiling panels of Siva and Parvati, Vishnu and Brahma. The other two date from the Rashtrakuta period.

Hucchappayya Math Beyond the Kunti Group is the Hucchappayya Math, dating to the seventh century, which has sculptures of amorous couples and their servants, while the beams inside are beautifully decorated. There is a tourist resthouse close to the temples should you wish to stay.

Pattadakal

On the banks of the Malaprabha River, Pattadakal – a World Heritage Site – was the second capital of the Chalukyan kings between the seventh and eighth centuries and the city where the kings were crowned. Ptolemy referred to it as 'Petrigal' in the first century AD. Two of their queens imported sculptors from Kanchipuram.

Most of the **temples** ⓘ *sunrise to sunset, foreigners Rs 250, Indians Rs 10*, cluster at the foot of a hill, built out of the pink-tinged gold sandstone, and display a succession of styles of the southern Dravida temple architecture of the Pallavas (even miniature scaled-down models) as well as the North Indian Nagara style, vividly illustrating the region's position at the crossroads of North and South Indian traditions. With one exception the temples are dedicated to Siva. Most of the site is included in the archaeological park. Megalithic monuments dating from the third to fourth centuries BC have also been found in the area.

Jambulinga and Kadasiddheshvara temples Immediately inside the entrance are the small eighth-century Jambulinga and Kadasiddheshvara temples. Now partly ruined, the curved towers survive and the shrine of the Jambulinga Temple houses a figure of the dancing Siva next to Parvati. The gateways are guarded by *dvarapalas*.

Galagnatha Temple Just to the east is the eighth-century Galaganatha Temple, again partly damaged, though its curved tower characteristic of North Indian temples is well preserved, including its *amalaka* on top. A relief of Siva killing the demon Andhaka is on the south wall in one of three original porches.

Sangamesvara Temple Dating from the reign of Vijayaditya (AD 696-733) this is the earliest temple. Although it was never completed it has all the hallmarks of a purely Dravidian style. Beautifully proportioned, the mouldings on the basement and pilasters divide the wall. The main shrine, into which barely any light is allowed to pass, has a corridor for circumambulation and a *lingam* inside. Above the sanctuary is a superbly proportioned tower of several storeys.

Kashi Vishveshvara Temple To the southwest is the late-eighth century North Indian-style Kashi Vishveshvara Temple, readily distinguishable by the *Nandi* in front of the porch. The interior of the pillared hall is richly sculpted, particularly with scenes of Krishna.

Virupaksha and Mallikarjuna temples The largest temples, the Virupaksha (AD 740-744) with its three-storey *vimana* and the Mallikarjuna (AD 745), typify the Dravida style, and were built in celebration of the victory of the Chalukyan king Vikramaditya II over the Pallavas at Kanchipuram by his wife, Queen Trailokyamahadevi. The king's death probably accounted for the fact that the **Mallikarjuna Temple** was unfinished, and you can only mark out some of the sculptures. However, the king's victory over the Pallavas enabled him to express his admiration for Pallava architecture by bringing back to Pattadakal one of the chief Pallava architects. The **Virupaksha**, a Shaivite temple, has a sanctuary surrounded by passageways and houses a black polished stone Siva *lingam*. A further Shaivite symbol is the huge 2.6-m-high chlorite stone *Nandi* at the entrance, contrasting with the pinkish sandstone surrounding it. The three-storey tower rises strikingly above the shrine, the outside walls of which, particularly those on the south side, are richly carved. Many show different forms of Vishnu and Siva, including some particularly striking panels which show Siva appearing out of a *lingam*. Note also the beautifully carved columns inside. They are very delicate, depicting episodes from the *Ramayana*, *Mahabharata* and the *Puranas*, as well as giving an insight into the social life of the Chalukyas. Note the ingenuity of the sculptor in making an elephant appear as a buffalo when viewed from a different side.

Jain temples In the ninth century the Rashtrakutas arrived and built a Jain temple with its two stone elephants a short distance from the centre. The carvings on the temples, particularly on the **Papanatha** near the village which has interesting sculpture on the ceiling and pillars, synthesizes North and South Indian architectural styles.

Badami → *Phone code: 08357. Population: 25,900.*

Badami occupies a dramatic site squeezed in a gorge between two high red sandstone hills. Once called Vatapi, after a demon, Badami was the Chalukyan capital from AD 543-757. The ancient city has several Hindu and Jain temples and a Buddhist cave and remains peaceful and charming. The transcendent beauty of the Hindu cave temples in their spectacular setting warrants a visit. The village with its busy bazar and a large lake has whitewashed houses clustered together along narrow winding lanes up the hillside. There are also scattered remains of 18 stone inscriptions (dating from the sixth to the 16th century).

The sites are best visited early in the morning. They are very popular with monkeys, which can be aggressive, especially if they see food. End the day by

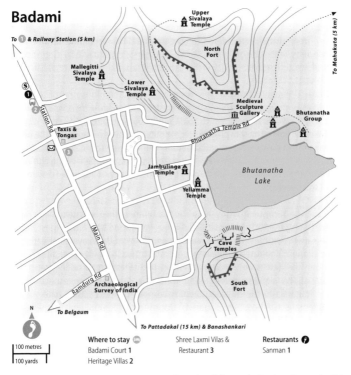

Badami

To ① & Railway Station (5 km)

To Mahakuta (5 km)

Upper Sivalaya Temple

North Fort

Mallegitti Sivalaya Temple

Lower Sivalaya Temple

Medieval Sculpture Gallery

Bhutanatha Group

Taxis & Tongas

Bhutanatha Temple Rd

Station Rd

Jambulinga Temple

Bhutanatha Lake

Yellamma Temple

Main Rd

Cave Temples

Ramdurg Rd

South Fort

Archaeological Survey of India

To Belgaum

N

100 metres
100 yards

To Pattadakal (15 km) & Banashankari

Where to stay 😴
Badami Court 1
Heritage Villas 2

Shree Laxmi Vilas & Restaurant 3

Restaurants 🍴
Sanman 1

watching the sun set from the eastern end of the tank. The area is well worth exploring by bicycle.

South Fort ⓘ *Foreigners Rs 100, Indians Rs 5.* The fort is famous for its cave temples, four of which were cut out of the hillside in the second half of the sixth century. There are 40 steps to **Cave 1**, the oldest. There are several sculpted figures, including Harihara, Siva and Parvati, and Siva as Nataraja with 18 arms seen in 81 dancing poses. **Cave 2**, a little higher than Cave 1, is guarded by *dvarapalas* (door keepers). Reliefs of Varaha and Vamana decorate the porch. **Cave 3**, higher still, is dedicated to Vishnu. According to a Kannada inscription (unique in Badami) it was excavated in AD 578. It has numerous sculptures including Narasimha (man-lion), Hari-Hara (Siva-Vishnu), a huge seated Vishnu and interesting friezes. Frescoes executed in the tempera technique are similar to that used in the Ajanta paintings, and so are the carved ceilings and brackets. **Cave 4**, probably about 100 years later than the three earlier caves, is the only Jain cave. It has a statue of the seated Parsvanatha with two *dvarapalas* at the entrance. The fort itself above the caves is closed to the public.

Buddhist Temple and Yellamma Temple The **Buddhist Temple** is in the natural cave close to the ancient artificial Bhutanatha Lake (Agasthya Lake), where the mossy green water is considered to cure illnesses. The **Yellamma Temple** has a female deity, while one of the two Shaivite temples is to Bhutanatha (God of souls); in this form, Siva appears angry in the dark inner sanctuary.

Mallegitti Sivalaya Temple This seventh-century temple is one of the finest examples of the early Southern style. It has a small porch, a *mandapa* (hall) and a narrower *vimana* (shrine), which Harle points out is typical of all early Western Chalukya temples. The slim pilasters on the outer walls are reminders of the period when wooden pillars were essential features of the construction. Statues of Vishnu and Siva decorate the outer walls, while animal friezes appear along the plinth and above the eaves. These are marked by a moulding with a series of ornamental small solid pavilions.

Jambulinga Temple An early temple in the centre of the town near the rickshaw stand. Dating from AD 699 as attested by an inscription and now almost hidden by houses, the visible brick tower is a late addition from the Vijayanagar period. Its three chapels, dedicated to Brahma, Vishnu and Siva, contain some fine carving, although the deities are missing and according to Harle the ceiling decoration already shows signs of deteriorating style. The carvings here, especially that of the Nagaraja in the outside porch, have helped to accurately date the Lad Khan Temple in Aihole (see page 94). Opposite the Jambulinga Temple is the 10th-century **Virupaksha Temple**.

North Fort temples ⓘ *Rs 2, take water with you.* These mainly seventh-century temples provide an insight into Badami's history. Steep steps, almost 1 m high, take you to 'gun point' at the top of the fort which has the remains of large granaries, a treasury and a watchtower. The **Upper Sivalaya Temple**, though damaged, still has some friezes and sculptures depicting Krishna legends. The North Fort was taken in a day by Colonel Munro in 1918, when he broke in through the east side.

An ancient **dolmen** site can be reached by an easy hike through interesting countryside; allow 3½ hours. A local English-speaking guide, Dilawar Badesha, at Tipu Nagar, charges about Rs 2.

Medieval Sculpture Gallery ⓘ *North of the tank, Sat-Thu 1000-1700, free.* Run by the Archaeological Survey, the gallery contains fine specimens from Badami, Aihole and Pattadakal and a model of the natural bridge at Sidilinapadi, 5 km away.

Mahakuta
Once reached by early pilgrims over rocky hills from Badami, 5 km away, Mahakuta is a beautiful complex of Chalukyan temples dating from the late seventh century and worth a detour. The superstructures reflect influences from both North and South India and one has an Orissan *deul*.

The restored temple complex of two dozen shrines dedicated to Siva is built around a large spring-fed tank within an enclosure wall. The old gateway to the southeast has fasting figures of Bhairava and Chamunda. On entering the complex, you pass the *Nandi* in front of the older **Mahakutesvara Temple** which has fine scrollwork and figures from the epics carved on the base. Larger Siva figures appear in wall niches, including an *Ardhanarisvara*. The temple is significant in tracing the development of the super-structure which began to externally identify the position of the shrine in Dravidian temples. Here the tower is dome-like and octagonal, the tiers supported by tiny 'shrines'. The **Mallikarjuna Temple** on the other side of the tank is similar in structure with fine carvings at the entrance and on the ceiling of the columned *mandapa* inside, depicting Hindu deities and *mithuna* couples. The enclosure has many smaller shrines, some carrying fine wall carvings. Also worth visiting is the **Naganatha Temple**, 2 km away.

Listings Cradle of hindu temple architecture *map p97*

Tourist information

Tourist office
Next to Mayura Chalukya, Badami, T08357-220414.

Where to stay

Badami
There is no formal money exchange but the **Mukambika** hotel, opposite the bus stand, may change small denominations of TCs.

$$$-$$ Badami Court
Station Rd, 2 km from town, T08357-720207.
It's a pleasant stroll to get there or take one of the frequent buses. 26 clean, modern, though cramped, rooms with bath (some a/c). There's a good restaurant, pool (small and only knee-

deep; non-residents Rs 80 per hr), gym and garden. It has a near monopoly on accommodation and service; maintenance reflects the absence of competition. Rates sometimes negotiable, only accepts rupees.

$$ Heritage Resort
Station Rd, T08357-220250, www.theheritage.co.in.
Smart and spacious rooms in handsome stone cottages, each with its own sit-out opening on to a green lawn. There's a vegetarian restaurant, and the staff can arrange transport and guides.

$ Shree Laxmi Vilas
Main Rd, T08357-220077.
Simple rooms, 3 with balconies with great views back to the temples. Right in the thick of it, so it's interesting but noisy.

Restaurants

Badami

$ Dhabas
Near the Tonga Stand.
Sells snacks.

$ Laxmi Vilas
Near the taxi stand.
Vegetarian meals.

$ Sanman
Near the bus stand.
Non-vegetarian dishes.

Festivals

Pattadakal
Jan **Nrutytsava** draws many famous dancers and is accompanied by a Craft Mela.
Mar-Apr **Temple car** festivals at Virupaksha and Mallikarjuna temples.

Transport

Badami
Bicycle
Bike hire from stalls along the main road, Rs 5 per hr; pleasant to visit Banashankari, Mahakuta and Pattadakal.

Bus
Few daily to **Hospet** (6 hrs), very slow and crowded but quite a pleasant journey with lots of stops; **Belgaum** via **Bagalkot** (4 hrs); **Bijapur**, 0645-0930 (4 hrs). Several to **Pattadakal** and **Aihole** from 0730. **Aihole** (2 hrs), from there to **Pattadakal** (1600). Last return bus from Aihole 1715, via Pattadakal.

Car
Hire from Badami with driver for Mahakuta, Aihole and Pattadakal, about Rs 650.

Train
The station is 5 km north on the **Bijapur–Gadag** line, with 6 trains daily in each direction (enquire about schedules); frequent buses to town.

The dry and undulating plains from Hospet to Bidar are broken by rocky outcrops providing superb sites for commanding fortresses, such as the one that sits in ruins overlooking Gulbarga. From 1347 to 1525 Gulbarga served as the first capital of the Bahmanis, but it is also widely known among South Indian Muslims as the home of Saiyid Muhammad Gesu Daraz Chisti (1320-1422) who was instrumental in spreading pious Islamic faith in the Deccan. The annual Urs festival in his memory can attract up to 100,000 people.

Sights

The town's sights and hotels are quite spread out so it is worth hiring an auto for half a day. The most striking remains in the town are the fort, with its citadel and mosque, the Jami Masjid, and the great tombs in its eastern quarter – massive, fortress-like buildings with their distinctive domes over 30 m high.

Fort ⓘ *1 km west of the centre of the present town.* Originally built by Ala-ud-din Bahmani in the 14th century, most of the outer structures and many of the buildings are in ruins. The outer door of the west gate and the *bala hissar* (citadel), a massive structure, however, remain almost intact although the whole place is very overgrown. A flight of ruined steps leads up to the entrance in the north wall; beware of dogs. It's easy to see why the Bahamis were so keen to upgrade their fortress. The fat fort walls at Gulbarga – romantically named as the 'bouquet of lovers' – may sit proud above the more modern artificial lake, and the *bala hissar* itself stands high with its plump rotund columns, but the whole is all too pregnable and modest. And there's no commanding hilltop to provide the impenetrability that the plateaux around Bidar bequeathed the dynasty's subsequent rulers.

All that remains of the palace structures are solitary walls stamped with arches, but the **Jami Masjid**, with its incongruous, uncanny likeness to the mosque at Córdoba in southern Spain, is both active and well maintained (similarities with the mosque at Córdoba have contributed to the legend that it was designed by a North African architect from the Moorish court). Beautiful geometrical angles of archways form as you walk under the 75 small roof domes zigzagging between the four corner domes. The whole area of 3500 sq m is covered by a dome over the *mihrab*, four corner domes and 75 minor domes, making it unique among Indian mosques. It was built by Firoz Shah Bahmani (1397-1432).

Tombs ⓘ *Note that women are not allowed to enter the tombs.* The tombs of the Bahmani sultans are in two groups. One lies 600 m to the west of the fort, the other on the east of the town. The latter have no remaining exterior decoration though the interiors show some evidence of ornamentation. The Dargah of the Chisti saint, **Hazrat Gesu Nawaz** – also known as Khwaja Bande Nawaz – who came to Gulbarga in 1413 during the reign of Firoz Shah Tughlaq, is open to visitors. The two-storey tomb with a highly decorated painted dome had a mother-of-pearl canopy added over the grave. The **Dargah library**, which has 10,000 books in Urdu, Persian and Arabic, is open to visitors.

The most striking of all the tombs near **Haft Gumbaz**, the eastern group, is that of **Taj-ud-Din Firuz** (1422). Unlike the other tombs it is highly ornate, with geometrical patterns developed in the masonry.

Listings Gulbarga

Where to stay

$ Aditya
Humnabad Rd, T08472-224040.
Reasonable rooms, some a/c with bath, clean vegetarian restaurant, very good value.

$ Pariwar
Humnabad Rd, near the station, T08472-221421, hotelpariwar@ yahoo.com.
Some a/c rooms, some cleaner and better value than others. Old but tidy, friendly staff and tasty vegetarian meals (no beer).

$ Santosh
University Rd (east of town), T08472-247991.

Some a/c rooms, good non-vegetarian restaurant (beer). The best in town.

Transport

Bus
There are bus connections to Hyderabad (190 km) and **Solapur**.

Train
Mumbai (CST): 8 trains daily, 13 hrs. **Bengaluru:** *Udayan Exp 6529,* 1900, 13½ hrs; *Lokmanya Tilak 1013,* 0905, 13 hrs. **Chennai (MC)**: *Chennai Exp 6011* (AC/II), 0130, 15 hrs; *Mumbai Chennai Mail 6009,* 1140, 18 hrs; *Dadar Chennai Exp 1063,* 0605, 14 hrs. **Hyderabad**: *Mumbai-Hyderabad Exp 7031* (AC/II), 0020, 5¾ hrs; *Hussainsagar Exp 7001,* 0740, 5 hrs.

Bidar → *Phone code: 08357. Population: 172,300.*

The scruffy bungalow town that is modern-day Bidar spreads out in a thin layer of buildings both within and outside of the imposing rust-red walls of the 15th-century fort that once played capital to two Deccan-ruling Muslim dynasties. The buildings may be new but there's still a medieval undercurrent to life here. Islam still grows sturdily: apart from the storehouses of government-subsidized industries to counter 'backwardness', the outskirts are littered with long white prayer walls to mop up the overspill from over-burdened mosques during Id. A few lone tiles, tucked into high corners, still cling to the laterite brick structures that stand in for the succession of immaculately made palaces which must once have glowed incandescent with bright blue, green and yellow designs. Elsewhere you can only see the outline of the designs. The old fort commands grand vistas across the empty cultivated land below. Each successive palace was ruined by invasions then built anew a little further east.

Sights

The intermingling of Hindu and Islamic architectural styles in the town has been ascribed to the use of Hindu craftsmen, skilled in temple carving in stone (particularly hornblende), who would have been employed by the succeeding Muslim rulers. They transferred their skill to Muslim monuments, no longer carving human figures, forbidden by Islam, but using the same technique to decorate with geometric patterns, arabesques and calligraphy, wall friezes, niches and borders.

Bidar

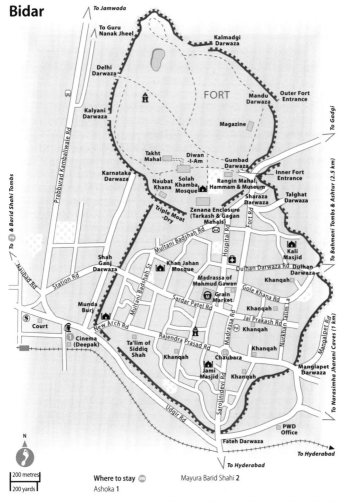

200 metres
200 yards

Where to stay
Ashoka 1   Mayura Barid Shahi 2

BACKGROUND

Bidar

The walled fort town, on a red laterite plateau in North Karnataka, once the capital of the **Bahmanis** and the **Barid Shahis**, remained an important centre until it fell to Aurangzeb in 1656. The Bahmani Empire fragmented into four kingdoms, and the ninth Bahmani ruler, **Ahmad Shah I**, shifted his capital from Gulbarga to Bidar in 1424, rebuilding the old Hindu fort to withstand cannon attacks, and enriching the town with beautiful palaces and gardens. With the decline of the Bahmanis, the Barid Shahi Dynasty founded here ruled from 1487 until Bidar was annexed to Bijapur in 1619.

The pillars, often of wood, were intricately carved and then painted and burnished with gold to harmonize with the encaustic tiles.

Inner Fort The Inner Fort, built by Muhammad Shah out of the red laterite and dark trapstone, was later embellished by Ali Barid. The steep hill to the north and east provided natural defence. It was protected to the south and west by a triple moat (now filled in). A series of gates and a drawbridge over the moat to the south formed the main entrance from the town. The second gate, the **Sharaza Darwaza** (1503) has tigers carved in bas relief on either side (Shia symbols of Ali as protector), the tile decorations on the walls and the *Nakkar Khana* (Drum gallery) above. Beyond this is a large fortified area which brings you to the third gate, the huge **Gumbad Darwaza**, probably built by Ahmad Shah Wali in the 1420s, which shows Persian influence. Note the decorated *gumbad* (dome).

You will see the triple moat to the right and after passing through the gateway, to your left are steps leading to the **Rangin Mahal** (Coloured Palace) where Muhammad Shah moved to, after finding the nearby Shah Burj a safe refuge in 1487 when the Abyssinians attacked. This small palace (an indication of the Bahmanis' declining years) was built by him, elaborately decorated with coloured tiles, later enhanced by Ali Barid with mother-of-pearl inlay on polished black granite walls as well as intricate wood carvings. If locked, ask at the museum (see below) for a key.

The old banyan tree and the **Shahi Matbak** (once a palace, but served as the Royal Kitchens) are to the west, with the **Shahi Hammam** (Royal Baths) next to it, which now houses a small **museum** ⓘ *0800-1700*. Exhibits include Hindu religious sculptures, Stone Age implements and cannon balls filled with bits of iron.

The **Lal Bagh**, where remains of water channels and a fountain witness to its former glory, and the *zenana*, are opposite the hammam. The **Sola Khamba** (16 columns) or **Zanani Mosque** is to the west (1423). The adjacent **Tarkash Mahal** (possibly refurbished by the Barid Shahis for the harem), to the south of Lal Bagh, is in ruins but still retains some tilework. From behind the mosque you can get to the **Gagan Mahal** (Heavenly Palace) that once carried fine decorations and is believed to have allowed the women to watch animal fights in the moat below from the back of the double hall. There's a good view from the roof. The **Diwan-i-Am** (Hall of Public Audience) is to the northwest of the *Zenana* which once held the *Takht-i-Firoza* (turquoise throne). To the north stands the **Takht Mahal** with royal apartments, audience hall and swimming baths. The steep staircase will take you down to underground chambers.

South of the Royal Apartments is the well that supplied water to the fort palaces through clay pipes. Of the so-called **Hazar** ('thousand') **Kothri** ⓘ *cycling is a good way of exploring the site, free,* you can only see a few underground rooms and passages which enabled a quick escape to the moat when necessary. Further south, the **Naubat Khana** probably housed the fort commander and the musicians. The road west from the Royal Apartments leads to the encircling Fort Wall (about 10 km) with bastions carrying vast cannons, the one to the northwest being the most impressive. You can see the ammunition magazine inside the **Mandu Darwaza** to the east before returning to the main fort entrance.

South of the Inner Fort As you walk south from the fort you can see the ruins of the **Madrassa of Mahmud Gawan** (1472). It is a fine example of his native Persian architecture and still bears signs of the once-brilliant green, white and yellow tiles which covered the whole façade with swirls of floral patterns and bold calligraphy.

The **Chaubara** is a 23-m circular watchtower at the crossroads, south of the town centre (good views from the top). South of this is the **Jami Masjid** (1430) which bears the Barid Shahis' typical chain and pendant motif. The **Kali Masjid** (1694), south of the Talghat Darwaza, is made of black trapstone. It has fine plaster decorations on the vaulted ceiling. There are also a number of **khanqahs** (monasteries).

Outside the fort The road east from the Dulhan Darwaza, opposite the General Hospital, leads to the eight **Bahmani tombs** ⓘ *Ashtur, 0800-1700, free, carry your own torch*. These are best seen in the morning when the light is better for viewing the interiors.

The square tombs, with arched arcades all round, have bulbous domes. The exteriors have stone carvings and superb coloured tile decoration showing strong Persian influence, while the interiors have coloured paintings with gilding. The **tomb of Ahmad Shah I**, the ninth Bahmani ruler, is impressive with a dome rising to nearly 35 m, and has a particularly fine interior with coloured decorations and calligraphy in the Persian style, highlighted with white borders. To the east and south are minor tombs of his wife and son. The **tomb of Alauddin Shah II** (1458) is possibly the finest. Similar in size to his father's, this has lost its fine painting inside but enough remains of the outer tilework to give an impression of its original magnificence.

On the way back is the **Chaukhandi of Hazrat Khalil-Ullah** which is approached by a flight of steps. Most of the tilework has disappeared but you can see the fine carvings at the entrance and on the granite pillars.

The **Barid Shahi tombs**, each of which once stood in its own garden, are on the Nanded Road to the west of the old town. That of **Ali Barid** is the most impressive, with the dome rising to over 25 m, with granite carvings, decorative plasterwork and calligraphy and floral patterns on the coloured tiles, which sadly can no longer be seen on the exterior. Here, abandoning the customary *mihrab* on the west wall, Ali Barid chose to have his tomb left open to the elements. It includes a prayer hall, music rooms, a combined tomb for his concubines and a pool fed by an aqueduct are nearby. There are fine carvings on the incomplete tomb to his son **Ibrahim Barid**, to the west. You can also see two sets of granite *ranakhambas* (lit battleposts) which may have been boundary markers. Other tombs show the typical arched niches employed to lighten the heavy walls which have decorative parapets.

The road north from Ali Barid's tomb descends to **Nanak Jhera**, where a *gurdwara* marks the holy place where Sikhs believe a miracle was performed by Guru Nanak and the *jhera* (spring) rose.

Listings Bidar *map p103*

Where to stay

There are several very basic hotels near Old Bus Station. A roadside Punjabi *dhaba* near the junction of NH9 and the Bidar Rd serves very good meals and is clean (including the toilet at the back).

$ Ashoka
Off Udgir Rd, near Deepak Cinema, T08482-223931.
A bit of a dive, but the best Bidar has to offer, friendly, with 21 clean, good-sized rooms, hot water, some a/c. The 'restaurant' is more of a drinking den.

$ Mayura Barid Shahi (KSTDC)
Opposite the New Bus Stand, T08482-228142.
Small but well-kept rooms, and some larger suites, with a good restaurant downstairs. A good deal for the price.

Shopping

Shops sell excellent *bidriwork*, particularly near the Ta'lim of Siddiq Shah. Craftsmen can be seen in the narrow lanes.

Transport

Auto-rickshaw
Easily available, Rs 15 being the going rate for most short hops across town.

Bicycle
Cycling is the best way to get around and see the sights. 'Cycle taxis' can be hired for Rs 20 per day from several outlets all over town and near the **New Bus Station**. You may have to ask a few before you find a shop that will rent to you, but persevere. Don't waste time with **Ganesh Cycle Taxi** near the New Bus Station.

Bus
There are services from the **New Bus Station**, 1 km west of centre, to most regional destinations, but check timings since the last bus is often quite early. From **Hyderabad** or **Gulburga** (under 4 hrs), or **Bijapur** (8 hrs). Private buses to **Mumbai**: 1700, 5 hrs, Rs 260. **Pune**: 1530, 3½ hrs, Rs 220. Taxi to **Gulburga** Rs 800.

Train
Bidar is on a branch line from Vikarabad to Parbhani Junction. Too slow to be of much use. **Aurangabad**: *Kacheguda-Manmad Exp 7664*, 2140, 8½ hrs. **Bengaluru**: *Hampi Link Exp 6593*, 1237, 18 hrs. **Secunderabad**: *Manmad-Kacheguda Exp 7663*, 0352, 5 hrs.

The main road from Hospet to Hyderabad passes through the important medieval centre of Raichur, once dominant in the Tungabhadra-Krishna *doab*, now an important but dusty market town, in the middle of a cotton-growing area.

The site of the fort's **citadel** at Raichur gives magnificent views over the vast open spaces of the Deccan plateau nearly 100 m below. Built in the mid-14th century Raichur became the first capital of the Bijapur Kingdom when it broke away from the Bahmani Sultans in 1489. Much of the fort itself is now in ruins, but there are some interesting remains. The **north gate** is flanked by towers, a carved elephant standing about 40 m away. On the inner walls are some carvings, and a tunnel reputedly built to enable soldiers access to barricade the gate in emergency. Near the **west gate** is the old palace. The climb to the citadel begins from near the north gate. In the citadel is a shrine with a row of cells with the **Jami Masjid** in the east. Its eastern gateway has three domes. The top of the citadel is barely 20 sq m.

There are some other interesting buildings in the fort below the hill, including the **Daftar ki Masjid** (Office Mosque), built around 1510 out of masonry removed from Hindu temples. It is one of the earliest mosques in the Deccan to be built in this way, with the bizarre result of producing flat ceilings with pillars carved for Chalukyan temples. The **Ek Minar ki Masjid** ('one-minaret mosque') is in the southeast corner of the courtyard. It has a distinctively Bahmani-style dome.

Background
Bengaluru

The region between the Tungabhadra and the Krishna rivers was home to some of the earliest settlements in peninsular India, dating back more than 500,000 years. By the Middle Stone Age there was already a regional division appearing between the black cotton soil area of the north and the granite-quartzite plateau of the south. In the north hunters used pebbles of jasper taken from riverbeds while quartz tools were developed to the south. The first agricultural communities of the peninsula have been identified in what is now northern Karnataka; radiocarbon dating puts the earliest of these settlements at about 3000 BC. Millet and gram were already widely grown by the first millennium BC and have remained staple crops ever since.

Karnataka has borne witness to a startling array of dynasties. Legend has it that India's first emperor, Chandragupta Maurya, became a Jain and renounced all worldly possessions, retiring to a cave at Sravanabelagola to meditate. The Western Gangas, from the third to 11th centuries, and the Banas, from the fourth to ninth centuries, controlled large parts of the region. The Chalukyas of central Karnataka took some of the lands between the Tungabhadra and Krishna rivers in the sixth century and built great temples in Badami. They vied with the powerful Rashtrakuta dynasty to unite the plateau and the coastal areas, while the Cholas of Tamil Nadu made incursions in the south and east. The break-up of the Chola Empire created a power vacuum in their former fiefdoms. In Karnataka the Hoysalas (11th-14th centuries) seized their chance, and left magnificent temples at their old capitals of Belur, Halebid and Somnathpur, exquisite symbols of their power and their religious authority. Then came the Sangama and Tuluva kings of the Vijayanagar Empire, which reached its peak in the mid-16th century with Hampi as its capital.

Karnataka was repeatedly in the frontline in the power struggle between Hindu and Muslim rulers. **Muhammad bin Tughlaq** attacked northern Karnataka in the 13th century, and during the Vijayanagar period the **Muslim sultanates** to the north continued to extend their influence. The Bidar period (1422-1526) of Bahmani rule was marked by wars with Gujarat and Malwa, continued campaigns against Vijayanagar, and expeditions against Orissa. **Mahmud Gawan**, the Wazir of the Bahmani sultanate, seized Karnataka between 1466 and 1481, and also took Goa, formerly guarded by Vijayanagar kings. By 1530 the kingdom had split into five independent sultanates. At times they came together to defend common interests, and in 1565 they co-operated to capture and kill the Vijayanagar ruler Rama Raya, going on to rout his army and ransack the capital at Hampi. But two of the sultanates, Bijapur and Golconda, gathered the lion's share of the spoils until the Mughals and British supplanted them.

South Karnataka saw a different succession of powers. While the Mughals were preoccupied fighting off the Marathas, the Hindu **Wodeyar** rulers of Mysore took control of Srirangapatnam and then Bangalore. They lost control to **Haidar Ali** in 1761, the opportunist commander-in-chief who joined forces with the French to extend his control westward to make Srirangapatnam his capital. The fierce Mysore Wars followed and with Haidar Ali's and then his son Tipu Sultan's death, the **British** restored the Wodeyars' rule in 1799. The Hindu royal family was still administering Mysore up until the reorganization of the states in the 1950s when the maharaja was appointed state governor.

Culture

A fault line runs through mainstream Kannada culture and politics, cleaving society into the northern Karnataka peasant caste, the **Lingayats**, and the **Vokkaligas** of the south. Lingayats follow the egalitarian and keen educationalist 12th-century saint Basavanna. The name Vokkaligas comes from 'okkalu', meaning to thresh, and these people are mostly farmers. The Kodavas from the southwest are a culture apart, physically fair and tall, worshippers of the goddess Cauvery and Lord Iguthappa. Karnataka has its share of tribal people. The nomadic Lambanis in the north and west are among several tribal peoples in the hill regions. The coastal region of Uttara Kannada is home to the Siddis, brought as slaves from southeast Africa, who retain the practice of ancestor worship, and the Navayats, from Saudi Arabia and Persia. The state has a significant Muslim minority of nearly seven million, and Mangalore particularly has a notable Catholic community.

Art and architecture

Karnataka's role as a border territory was illustrated in the magnificent architecture of the Chalukyan Dynasty from AD 450 to AD 650. Here, notably in Aihole, were the first stirrings of *Brahman* temple design. Relics show the parallel development of Dravidian and North Indian temple architecture: in Pattadakal alone there are four temples built on North Indian *Nagari* principles and six built on South Indian *Dravida* lines. Belur, Halebid and Somnathpur's star-shaped bases, bell-towered shrines and exquisite carvings represent a distinctive combination of both traditions. The Vijayanagara kings advanced temple architecture to blend in with the rocky, boulder-ridden landscape at Hampi. Bijapur has some of the finest Muslim monuments on the Deccan from the austere style of the Turkish rulers to the refinement in some of the pavilions and the world's second largest dome at the Gol Gumbaz.

Dance, drama and music

Open-air folk theatre or *Bayalata* grew from religious ritual and is performed in honour of the local deity. Actors improvise their plays on an informal stage. Performances usually start at night and often last into the early hours. The famous *Yakshagana* or *Parijata* tends to have just one narrator while other forms have four or five, assisted by a jester. The plots of the *Dasarata* (which enacts several stories) and *Sannata* (which elaborates one theme) are drawn from mythology but sometimes highlight real-life incidents. The *Doddata* is less refined than the *Yakshagana* but they have much in common, beginning with a prayer to the god Ganesh, using verse, and drawing from the stories of the epics *Ramayana* and *Mahabharata*. The costumes are elaborate with fantastic stage effects, loud noises and war cries and vigorous dances.

Government

The 19 districts are grouped into four divisions – Bengaluru, Mysore, Belgaum and Gulbarga. Caste rivalry between Vokkaligas and Lingayats remains a powerful factor and faction fighting within parties is a recurrent theme. In 2004, Congress suffered a swinging backlash against its liberal economic policies that had fuelled Bengaluru's rise to become the darling of the IT and biotechnology industries. The right-wing BJP (Bharatiya Janata Party, or Indian People's Party) became the largest single party in the Assembly, though it was initially prevented from forming government by a short-lived coalition between Congress and the secular Janata Dal party.

The BJP finally took power in its own right in 2008 under Lingayat leader BS Yeddyurappa. The party's reign was tarred with accusations of corruption and nepotism – several senior ministers served jail time for scams, including Yeddyurappa himself – and its woes were compounded by three leadership coups in five years. In 2013, to a background of unease about the BJP's push towards 'saffronization' (where Hindu cultural history is glorified to the detriment of more recent Islamic or Christian traditions) of public life in the state, Karnataka's voters overwhelmingly reinstalled the Congress party under the leadership of avowed atheist Siddaramaiah.

Economy

Karnataka is one of India's most rapidly modernizing states, and an undisputed leader in IT skills, biotech and industrial activity. Based on its early development of aeronautics and high precision machine tools, Bengaluru has become a world centre for the computer industry, receiving a much-quoted seal of approval from Bill Gates. Outside the cities, agriculture and forestry remain important. Demand for irrigation is growing rapidly against a backdrop of frequent droughts. The water issue is the cause of escalating tension with neighbouring Tamil Nadu, a conflict that plays out at the top political level, with a verdict reached by the Indian Supreme Court to allocate resources in 2007, and as a trigger for mass demonstrations, rallies have led to violent clashes against Tamilian interests, property and people within Karnataka's borders.

Practicalities
Bengaluru

Getting there

Air

India is accessible by air from virtually every continent and, thanks to a handful of direct flights and excellent connections via the Gulf and Southeast Asia, it's possible to fly straight into Bengaluru, rather than come via the usual international gateways of Mumbai and Delhi.

Karnataka itself boasts two international airports: **Bengaluru** and **Mangalore** – though the latter only has limited services from the Middle East – and there are also convenient gateways in neighbouring states, such as Chennai, Hyderabad, Goa, Kochi and Kozhikode. Several carriers permit 'open-jaw' travel, making it possible to fly into one airport and out of another – a great option if you want to explore far-flung corners of Karnataka without having to backtrack to your point of arrival.

The cheapest return flights to Bengaluru from London start at around £350 but leap to £800+ as you approach the high seasons of Christmas, New Year and Easter.

From Europe

Despite being India's third busiest airport, Bengaluru still receives relatively few direct flights from Europe, with only **British Airways**, **Air France** and **Lufthansa** offering direct flights. You'll get more options, and potentially cheaper prices, flying via Mumbai or Delhi; **Air India** and **Jet Airways** fly to both airports from several cities in mainland Europe, while Delhi in particular is well served by European flag carriers including **Austrian**, **Finnair**, **KLM** and **Swiss**, as well as those mentioned above.

It can be substantially cheaper, and often more convenient, to fly to Karnataka with Middle Eastern airlines, transiting via airports in the Gulf. Several airlines (including **Emirates**, **Etihad**, **Qatar** and **Oman Air**) offer good fares from a wide choice of British and European airports to Bengaluru via their hub cities. This may add a couple of hours to the journey time, but allows you to avoid the more fraught route via Mumbai, which involves long immigration queues and shuttling from the international to the domestic terminal. Consolidators in the UK can quote some competitive fares; these include www.ebookers.com, and **North South Travel** ⓘ T01245-608291, www.northsouthtravel.co.uk (profits to charity). Search engines such as www.momondo.co.uk, www.kayak.co.uk and www.skyscanner.net, can show heavily discounted fares on offer from third-party ticket agents, but be careful to check reviews for the agent before buying; some of the cheapest ticket sellers attract a large number of complaints.

From North America

From the east coast, several airlines including **Air India**, **Jet Airways** and **Delta** fly from New York to Mumbai, from where you can pick up an internal flight to Bengaluru or Mangalore. However, as with Europe, the best deals are often from carriers based in the Gulf. From the west coast, your best option is to fly to Bengaluru via Hong Kong, Singapore, Seoul or Bangkok using one of those countries' national carriers. **Air Canada** operates between Vancouver and Delhi. **STA** ⓘ *www.statravel.co.uk*, has offices in many US cities, Toronto and Ontario. Student fares are also available from **Travel Cuts** ⓘ *www.travelcuts.com*, in Canada. **Momondo.com** is one of the best online-only sources of cheap flights, or check out **www.flightfox.com**, an online community of flight experts who can hack together airfares substantially cheaper than those available even from online agents.

From Australasia

Qantas, **Singapore Airlines**, **Thai Airways**, **Malaysian Airlines**, **Cathay Pacific** and **Air India** are the principal airlines connecting the continents, although none have direct flights to the south. If you're touring South India, **Singapore Airlines** offers the most flexibility, with flights to Bengaluru as well as connections to Kochi and Thiruvananthapuram through its subsidiary **Silk Air**. Low-cost carriers, including **Air Asia** (via Kuala Lumpur), **Scoot** and **Tiger Airways** (Singapore), also offer flights to Bengaluru at substantial savings, though long layovers and possible missed connections make this a potentially more risky venture than flying with the mainstream airlines. **STA** and **Flight Centre** offer discounted tickets from their branches in major cities in Australia and New Zealand. On the web, **www.adioso. com** allows you to search for flights to all of India, and search results include hacker deals using budget airlines.

Airport information

The formalities on arrival in India have been increasingly streamlined during the last few years and the facilities at the major international airports greatly improved. However, arrival can still be a slow process. Disembarkation cards, with an attached customs declaration, are handed out to passengers during the inward flight. The immigration form should be handed in at the immigration counter on arrival. The customs slip will be returned, for handing over to customs officials on leaving the baggage collection hall. You may well find that there are delays of over an hour at immigration in processing passengers who need help with filling in forms. When departing, note that you'll need to have a printout of your itinerary to get into the airport, and the security guards will only let you into the terminal within three hours of your flight. Many airports require you to scan your bags before checking in and in rare cases you may also be asked to identify your checked luggage after going through immigration and security checks.

Departure charges

Several Indian airports have begun charging a Passenger Service Fee or User Development Fee to each departing passenger. This is normally included in international tickets, but some domestic airlines have been reluctant to incorporate the charge. Keep some spare cash in rupees in case you need to pay the fee on arriving at the terminal.

Getting around

Air

India has a comprehensive flight network linking the major cities of the different states. **Bengaluru** is one of the country's most important domestic hubs and has frequent flight connections with major cities throughout India, as well as regional airports within Karnataka such as **Mangalore** and **Hubli**. Deregulation of the airline industry has had a transformative effect on travel within India, with a host of low-budget private carriers jockeying to provide the lowest prices or highest frequency on popular routes. On any given day, booking a few days in advance, you can expect to fly between Mumbai and Bengaluru for around US$100 one way including taxes, while booking a month in advance can reduce the price to US$50-60.

Although it is comparatively expensive and delays and re-routing can be irritating, flying is an option worth considering for covering vast distances or awkward links on a route.

The best way to get an idea of the current routes, carriers and fares is to use a third-party booking website such as www.cheapairticketsindia.com (toll-free numbers: UK T0800-101 0928, USA T1-888 825 8680), www.cleartrip.com, www.makemytrip.co.in, or www.yatra.com. Booking with these is a different matter: some refuse foreign credit cards outright, while others have to be persuaded to give your card special clearance. Tickets booked on these sites are typically issued as an email ticket or an SMS text message – the simplest option if you have an Indian mobile phone. At the time of writing, **Makemytrip** and **Cheapairtickets** were definitely accepting non-Indian credit cards.

Road

Road travel is often the only choice for reaching many places. For the uninitiated, travel by road can also be a worrying experience because of the apparent absence of conventional traffic regulations; mountain roads can be unnerving, especially during the rainy season when landslides are possible. Vehicles drive on the left – in theory. Routes around the major cities are usually crowded with lorry traffic, especially at night, and the main roads are often poor and slow. There are a few motorway-style expressways – the toll road leading from Bengaluru airport towards the city is deceptively wide, fast and carpet-like – but most main roads are single track. Some district roads are quiet and, although they are not fast, they can be a good way of seeing the country and village life if you have the time.

Bus

Buses now reach virtually every part of India, offering a cheap, if often uncomfortable, means of visiting places off the rail network. Very few villages are now more than 2-3 km from a bus stop. Most services in Karnataka are operated by the government-run **Karnataka State Road Transport Corporation (KSRTC)**

ⓘ *www.ksrtc.in*. These buses depart from the central bus stand in every town. Larger towns and popular tourist destinations are also served by private bus operators, whose offices cluster around the main bus stand. The more upmarket government buses, and most private operators, are a little bit more expensive but have fewer stops and are a bit more comfortable. They also allow advance reservations online, including printable e-tickets (check **www.redbus.in** and **www.viaworld.in**). There are also many sleeper buses (a contradiction in terms); if you must take a sleeper bus, choose a lower berth near the front of the bus. The upper berths are almost always really uncomfortable.

Bus categories Though comfortable for sightseeing trips, apart from the very best 'sleeper coaches' even **air-conditioned luxury coaches** can be very uncomfortable for really long journeys. Often the air conditioning is very cold so wrap up. Journeys over 10 hours can be extremely tiring so it is better to go by train if there is a choice. **Express buses** run over long distances (frequently overnight), these are often called 'video coaches' and can be an appalling experience unless you appreciate loud film music blasting through the night. Ear plugs and eye masks may ease the pain. They rarely average more than 45 kph. **Local buses** are often crowded, bumpy, slow and usually poorly maintained. However, over short distances, they can be a very cheap, friendly and easy way of getting about. Even where signboards are not in English someone will usually give you directions. Many larger towns have **minibus** services which charge a little more than the buses and pick up and drop passengers on request. Again very crowded, and with restricted headroom, they are the fastest way of getting about many of the larger towns.

Bus travel tips Some towns have different bus stations for different destinations. Booking on major long-distance routes is now computerized. Book in advance where possible and avoid the back of the bus where it can be very bumpy. If your destination is only served by a local bus you may do better to take the Express bus and 'persuade' the driver, with a tip in advance, to stop where you want to get off. You will have to pay the full fare to the first stop beyond your destination but you will get there faster and more comfortably. When an unreserved bus pulls into a bus station, there is usually an unholy scramble for seats, whilst those arriving have to struggle to get off! In many areas there is an unwritten 'rule of reservation' using handkerchiefs or bags thrust through the windows to reserve seats. Some visitors may feel a more justified right to a seat having fought their way through the crowd, but it is generally best to do as local people do and be prepared with a handkerchief or sarong. As soon as it touches the seat, it is yours! Leave it on your seat when getting off to use the toilet at bus stations.

Car

A car provides a chance to travel off the beaten track, and gives unrivalled opportunities for seeing something of India's great variety of villages and small towns. Until recently, the most widely used hire car was the romantic but notoriously unreliable Hindustan Ambassador. You can still find them for hire in parts of Karnataka, but they're gradually giving way to more efficient (and boring) Tata and Toyota models with mod cons such as air-conditioning ... and seat belts. A handful of international agencies offer self-drive car hire (**Avis**, **Sixt**), but India's majestically anarchic traffic culture is not for the faint-hearted, and emphatically not a place for those who value such quaint concepts as lane discipline, or indeed driving on an assigned side of the road. It's much more common, and comfortable, to hire not just the car but someone to drive it for you.

Car hire If you fancy the idea of being Lady Penelope and gadding about with your own chauffeur, dream no more. Hiring a car and driver is the most comfortable and efficient way to cover short to medium distances, and although prices have increased sharply in recent years, car travel in India is still a bargain by Western standards. Even if you're travelling on a modest budget, a day's car hire can help take the sting out of an arduous journey, allowing you to go sightseeing along the way without looking for somewhere to stash your bags.

Local drivers often know their way around an area much better than drivers from other states, so where possible it is a good idea to get a local driver who speaks the state language, in addition to being able to communicate with you. The best way to guarantee a driver who speaks good English is to book in advance with a professional travel agency, either in India or in your home country. Recommended operators with English speaking drivers include **Arjun Tours** ⓘ www.arjuntours. com, and **Skyway** ⓘ www.skywaytour.com. You can, if you choose, arrange car hire informally by asking around at taxi stands, but don't expect your driver to speak anything more than rudimentary English.

On pre-arranged overnight trips the fee you pay will normally include fuel and inter-state taxes – check before you pay – and a wage for the driver. Drivers are responsible for their expenses, including meals (and the pervasive servant-master culture in India means that most will choose to sit separately from you at meal times). Some tourist hotels provide rooms for drivers, but they often choose to sleep in the car overnight to save money. In some areas drivers also seek to increase their earnings by taking you to hotels and shops where they earn a handsome commission; these are generally hugely overpriced and poor alternatives to the hotels recommended in this book, so don't be afraid to say no and insist on your choice of accommodation. If you feel inclined, a tip at the end of the tour of Rs 100 per day is perfectly acceptable.

	Tata Indica non-a/c	Tata Indigo non-a/c	Hyundai Accent a/c	Toyota Innova
8 hrs/80 km	Rs 1200	Rs 1600	Rs 2200	Rs 2500
Extra km	Rs 8	Rs 10	Rs 15	Rs 15
Extra hr	Rs 80	Rs 100	Rs 200	Rs 180
Out of town				
Per km	Rs 8	Rs 10	Rs 15	Rs 15
Night halt	Rs 200	Rs 200	Rs 300	Rs 250

Taxi

Taxi travel in India is a great bargain, and in most cities in Karnataka you can take a taxi from the airport to the centre for under US$15.

Yellow-top taxis in cities and large towns are metered, although tariffs change frequently. The latest rates are typically shown on a fare conversion chart which should be read in conjunction with the meter reading. Increased night-time rates apply in most cities, and there might be a small charge for luggage.

Insist on the taxi meter being flagged in your presence. If the driver refuses, the official advice is to contact the police. When a taxi doesn't have a meter, you will need to fix the fare before starting the journey; ask at your hotel desk for a rough price. As a foreigner, it is rare to get a taxi in the big cities to use the meter – if they are eager to, watch out as sometimes the meter is rigged and they have a fake rate card. Also, watch out for the David Blaine-style note shuffle: you pay with a Rs 500 note, but they have a Rs 100 note already in their hand.

Most airports and many major stations have booths where you can book a prepaid taxi. For slightly more than the metered fare these allow you to sidestep overcharging and give you the security of knowing that your driver will take you to your destination by the most direct route. You might be able to join up with other travellers at the booth to share a taxi to your hotel or a central point. It's OK to give the driver a small tip at the end of the journey.

At night, always have a clear idea of where you want to go and insist on being taken there. Taxi drivers may try to convince you that the hotel you have chosen 'closed three years ago' or is 'completely full'. Say that you have a reservation.

Rickshaw

Auto-rickshaws (autos) are almost universally available in towns across Karnataka and are the cheapest and most convenient way of getting about. It is best to walk a short distance away from a hotel gate before picking up an auto to avoid paying an inflated rate. In addition to using them for short journeys it is often possible to hire them by the hour, or for a half or full day's sightseeing. In some areas younger drivers who speak some English and know their local area well may want to show you around. However, rickshaw drivers are often paid a commission by hotels, restaurants and gift shops so advice is not always impartial. Drivers generally refuse to use the meter – though in Bengaluru meter use is now standard. If you have real problems it can help to note down the vehicle licence number and threaten to go to the police. If you're planning trips around Bengaluru or Mysore, www.meterpodu.in gives a good idea of what the fare should be by showing how much other users have paid for similar journeys.

Cycle-rickshaws and **horse-drawn tongas** are more common in the more rustic setting of a small town or the touristy parts of a large one. You will need to fix a price by bargaining. The animal attached to a *tonga* usually looks too undernourished to have the strength to pull the driver, let alone passengers.

Train

Trains can still be the cheapest and most comfortable means of travelling long distances; overnight journeys also save on hotel expenses. Passengers have access to Railway Retiring Rooms, which can be useful from time to time. Above all, it provides an ideal opportunity to meet local travellers and catch a glimpse of life on the ground.

High-speed trains

Shatabdi Express trains connect Bengaluru with Mysore and Chennai. A clear step up from the stumblebum pace of the average Indian train, they reliably depart and arrive on time, and stops en route are limited to major stations. **Rajdhani ('Capital City') Express** trains are similarly efficient for long-distance overnight travel (trains connect Bengaluru with New Delhi and Kolkata), while **Duronto Express** trains are less frequent but the fastest of the lot, running between Bengaluru and Delhi non-stop. Due to high demand these trains need to be booked well in advance (up to 60 days). Meals and drinks are usually included.

Classes

A/c First Class, available only on main routes, is the choice of the Indian upper crust, with two- or four-berth carpeted sleeper compartments with washbasin. As with all air-conditioned sleeper accommodation, bedding is included, and the windows are tinted to the point of being almost impossible to see through. **A/c Sleeper**, two- and three-tier configurations (known as 2AC and 3AC), are clean and comfortable and popular with middle-class families; these are the safest carriages for women travelling alone. **A/c Executive Class**, with wide reclining seats, are available on many Shatabdi trains at double the price of the ordinary **a/c Chair Car** which are equally comfortable. **First Class (non-a/c)** is gradually being phased out, and is now restricted to a handful of routes through Karnataka, but the run-down old carriages still provide a very enjoyable combination of privacy and windows that can open. **Second Class (non-a/c)** two- and three-tier (commonly called **Sleeper**) provides exceptionally cheap and atmospheric travel, with basic padded vinyl seats and open windows that allow the sights and sounds of India (not to mention dust, insects and flecks of spittle expelled by passengers up front) to drift into the carriage. On long journeys Sleeper can be crowded and uncomfortable, and toilet facilities can be unpleasant; it is nearly always better to use the Indian-style squat loos rather than the Western-style ones as they are better maintained. At the bottom rung is **Unreserved Second Class**, with hard wooden benches. You can travel long distances for a trivial amount of money, but unreserved carriages are often ridiculously crowded, and getting off at your station may involve a battle of will and strength against the hordes trying to shove their way on.

Indrail passes

These allow travel across the entire Indian railway network, but you have to spend a high proportion of your time on the train to make it worthwhile. However, the

TRAVEL TIP

Train touts

Many railway stations – and some bus stations and major tourist sites – are heavily populated with touts. Self-styled 'agents' will board trains before they enter the station and seek out tourists, often picking up their luggage and setting off with words such as "Madam!/Sir! Come with me madam/sir! You need top-class hotel …". They will even select porters to take your luggage without giving you any say.

If you have succeeded in getting off the train or even in obtaining a trolley you will find hands eager to push it for you.

For a first-time visitor such touts can be more than a nuisance. You need to keep calm and firm. Decide in advance where you want to stay. If you need a porter on trains, select one yourself and agree a price before the porter sets off with your baggage. If travelling with a companion one can stay guarding the luggage while the other finds a taxi and negotiates the price to the hotel. It sounds complicated and sometimes it feels it. The most important thing is to behave as if you know what you are doing!

advantages of pre-arranged reservations and automatic access to Foreign Tourist Quota tickets can tip the balance in favour of the pass for some travellers.

Tourists (foreigners and Indians resident abroad) may buy these passes from the tourist sections of principal railway booking offices and pay in foreign currency, major credit cards, traveller's cheques or rupees with encashment certificates. For a full list of fares see www.indianrail.gov.in/international_tourist.html.

Indrail passes can also conveniently be bought abroad from special agents. For people contemplating a single long journey soon after arriving in India, the half- or one-day pass with a confirmed reservation is worth the peace of mind; two- or four-day passes are also sold.

The UK agent is **SDEL** ⓘ *103 Wembley Park Dr, Wembley, Middlesex HA9 8HG, UK, T020-8903 3411, www.indiarail.co.uk*, which makes all necessary reservations and offers excellent advice. It can also book **Air India** and **Jet Airways** internal flights.

Cost

A/c First Class costs about double the rate for two-tier shown below, and non a/c Sleeper class about half. Children (aged five to 12) travel at half the adult fare. Young people (12-30 years) and senior citizens (65 years and over) are allowed a 30% discount on journeys over 500 km (just show your passport).

Period	US$ A/c 2-tier	Period	US$ A/c 2-tier
½ day	26	21 days	198
1 day	43	30 days	248
7 days	135	60 days	400
15 days	185	90 days	530

Fares for individual journeys are based on distance covered and reflect both the class and the type of train. Higher rates apply on the Mail and Express trains and the air-conditioned Shatabdi and Rajdhani expresses.

Internet services

Official sources for train-related information include www.railtourismindia.com, www.indianrail.gov.in, www.erail.in and www.trainenquiry.com, where you can check timetables (which change frequently), numbers, seat availability and even the running status of your train. Internet e-tickets can be bought and printed at www.irctc.in, though it's a fiendishly frustrating system to use, and paying with a foreign credit card is fraught with difficulty. If you plan to do a lot of train travel on popular routes it might be worth the effort to get your credit card recognized by the booking system. This process changes often, so your best option is to consult the very active India transport forums at www.indiamike.com.

Even more useful than the official sites is www.inidarailinfo.com, which has all the timetable info you could want, plus deep statistics on how late you can expect to arrive, and an individual forum for each train where users comment on everything from the standard of cleanliness to the quality of catering.

Tickets and reservations

It is possible to reserve tickets for virtually any train on the network from one of the 3000-plus computerized reservation centres across India. It is always best to book as far in advance as possible (usually up to 60 days). To reserve a seat on a particular train, note down the train's name, number and departure time and fill in a reservation form while you line up at the ticket window; you can use one form for up to four passengers. At busy stations the wait can take an hour or more.

You can save a lot of time and effort by asking a travel agent to get your tickets for a fee of Rs 50-100. If the class you want is full, ask if tickets are available under any of Indian Rail's special quotas. **Foreign Tourist Quota** (FTQ) reserves a small number of tickets on popular routes for overseas travellers; you need your passport and either an exchange certificate or ATM receipt showing your bank balance to book tickets under FTQ. The other useful special quota is **Tatkal**, which releases a last-minute pool of tickets at 1000 on the day before the train departs; you have to book them in person at a reservation centre.

If the quota system can't help you, consider buying a 'wait list' ticket, as seats often become available close to the train's departure time; phone the station on the day of departure to check your ticket's status. If you don't have a reservation for a particular train but carry an Indrail Pass, you may get one by arriving three hours early. Be wary of touts at the station offering tickets, hotels or exchange.

Timetables

It's best to consult the websites listed above for the most up-to-date timetable information. Once you're on the ground, regional timetables are available cheaply from station bookstalls; the monthly *Indian Bradshaw* is sold in principal stations, and the handy but daunting *Trains at a Glance* (Rs 40) lists popular trains likely to be used by most foreign travellers. You can pick it up in the UK from SDEL (see page 120).

Where to stay

India has an enormous range of accommodation, and you can stay safely and very cheaply by Western standards right across the country. The mainstay of the budget traveller is the ubiquitous Indian 'business hotel'. These are usually within walking distance of train and bus stations, anonymous but generally decent value, with en suite rooms of hugely variable cleanliness and a TV showing 110 channels of cricket and *Bollywood MTV*. At the top end, alongside international chains like **ITC Sheraton** (ostentatious) and **Radisson Blu** (dependable), India boasts several home-grown hotel chains, the best of which are the **Taj** group with its exceptional heritage and palace hotels; and the luxurious rural resorts run by **Orange County** ⓘ *www.orangecounty.in*.

Karnataka hasn't jumped aboard the heritage guesthouse bandwagon as enthusiastically as neighbouring Kerala, but rural corners of the state offer plenty of opportunities to stay in style in converted mansions, plush plantation bungalows. Along the Karavalli coast you'll also find a huge variety of individual lodgings, from porous coconut-fibre beach shacks that don't even come with a lock, to luxurious resorts overlooking the Arabian Sea and minimalist Zen retreats hidden in paddy fields. Meanwhile in Hampi, the backpackers headquarters of Karnataka, you'll find any number of small and simple rooms in family guesthouses, with not much more than a bed and a mosquito net (and maybe your own bathroom), on offer for a few hundred rupees a night.

In the high season (October to April, peaking at Christmas/New Year and again at Easter) bookings can be heavy in popular destinations such as Coorg, Kabini, Hampi and Gokarna. It is generally possible to book in advance by phone, fax or email, sometimes on payment of a deposit, but double check your reservation a day or two beforehand and always try to arrive as early as possible in the day to iron out any problems.

Price codes

Where to stay	Restaurants
$$$$ over US$150	$$$ over US$12
$$$ US$66-150	$$ US$6-12
$$ US$30-65	$ under US$6
$ under US$30	

For a double room in high season, excluding taxes.

For a two-course meal for one person, excluding drinks and service charge.

Hotels

Price categories The category codes used in this book are based on prices of double rooms excluding taxes. They are not star ratings and individual facilities vary considerably. Modest hotels may not have their own restaurant but will often offer 'room service', bringing in food from outside; in temple towns, restaurants may only serve vegetarian food.

Off-season rates Large reductions are made by hotels in all categories during low season. Always ask if a discount is available. You may also request the 10-15% agent's commission to be deducted from your bill if you book direct. Clarify whether the agreed figure includes all taxes.

Taxes Hotel rooms costing Rs 500 or above are usually subject to a combined Luxury and Service Tax of 19.4%. Taxes are not necessarily payable on meals, so it is worth settling your meals bill separately. Most hotels in the $$ category and above accept payment by credit card. Check your final bill carefully; visitors have complained of incorrect bills, even in the most expensive hotels. The problem particularly afflicts groups, when last-minute extras appear mysteriously on some guests' bills. Check the evening before departure, and keep all receipts.

Hotel facilities Be prepared for difficulties that are rarely encountered in the West. It is best to inspect the room and check that all equipment (air conditioning, TV, water heater, toilet flush) works before checking in at a modest hotel. Many hotels try to wring too many years' service out of their linen, and it's quite common to find sheets that are stained, frayed or riddled with holes. Don't expect any but the most expensive or tourist-savvy hotels to fit a top sheet to the bed.

In some areas **power cuts** are common, or hot water may be restricted to certain times of day. The largest hotels have their own generators but it is best to carry a good torch.

In some regions **water supply** is rationed periodically. Keep a bucket filled to use for flushing the toilet during water cuts. Occasionally, tap water may be discoloured due to rusty tanks. During the cold weather and in hill stations, hot water will be available at certain times of day, sometimes in buckets, but is usually very restricted in quantity. Electric water heaters may provide enough for a shower but not enough to fill a bath tub. » *For details on drinking water, see page 126.*

Hotels close to temples can be very **noisy**, especially during festivals. Music blares from loudspeakers late at night and from very early in the morning, often making sleep impossible. Mosques call the faithful to prayers at dawn. Some find ear plugs helpful.

Some hotels offer **24-hour checkout**, meaning you can keep the room for a full 24 hours from the time you arrive – a great option if you arrive in the afternoon and want to spend the morning sightseeing.

Homestays

At the upmarket end, increasing numbers of travellers are keen to stay in private homes and guesthouses, opting not to book large hotel chains that keep you at arm's length from a culture. Instead, travellers get home-cooked meals in heritage houses and learn about a country through conversation with often fascinating hosts. In Karnataka, Coorg and Chikmagalur are the homestay hotspots – though note that 'homestay' is a widely abused term, and not all places marketed as such will offer the home-and-family atmosphere you might expect. Companies specializing in homestays include **MAHout** ⓘ *www.mahoutuk.com*, and **Travel Malnad** ⓘ *www.travelmalnad.com*. **Karnataka Tourism** has a list of registered homestays, though no detailed information or pictures, on their website at www.karnatakatourism.org/homestay.

RESPONSIBLE TRAVEL
Plastic water bottles

There is growing concern over the mountains of plastic bottles that are collecting and the waste of resources needed to produce them, so travellers are being encouraged to use alternative methods of getting safe drinking water. Many hotels and restaurants provide drinking water purified using a combination of ceramic and carbon filters, chlorine and UV irradiation. Ask for 'filter water'; if the water tastes vaguely like a swimming pool it is probably quite safe to drink, though it's best to introduce your system gradually to the new water. A portable water filter is a good idea, carrying the drinking water in a plastic bottle in an insulated carrier. Always carry enough drinking water with you when travelling. It is important to use pure water for cleaning teeth.

Food & drink

Food

You'll find just as much variety in dishes crossing South India as you would on an equivalent journey across Europe. Varying combinations of spices and unique local ingredients give each region its distinctive flavour. Yet for most people, the mention of South Indian food calls to drooling recollection the dishes of Karnataka, more specifically those that emanate from the coastal temple town of Udupi.

Catering for the strict vegetarian needs of Krishna's devotees, Udupi food has spread far and wide around India. Classic dishes include *idli* (fluffy steamed cakes of rice flour) and *vada* (a crispy deep-fried doughnut riddled with peppercorns and chilli); both are served with the ever-present spicy gravy called *sambar*. For a less spicy introduction to the day, try *upma* or *uppittu* (a thick savoury porridge of semolina, chilli and coriander), and *kesari bath* or *sheera* (a sweet equivalent made with saffron, jaggery and raisins); mix the two together and you have *chow chow bath*, possibly the ultimate sweet-and-salty breakfast treat. Every town in the state has a slew of places serving these staples, invariably washed down with delicious milky-sweet South Indian filter coffee, and for less than US$1 you can fuel yourself up for a full morning's sightseeing.

The iconic Udupi dish is the *dosa*, a wafer thin pancake made from rice and lentil flour – or less commonly from *rava* (semolina) – which can be served plain or masala-style, stuffed with a turmeric-laden mix of onion, potato and chilli; the Mysore variant adds a thin layer of red garlic-chilli chutney. A good *dosa*, served hot off the *tawa* in a dingy old café with accompanying coconut and coriander chutney and *sambar*, is enough to bring a grown man to tears; the first snap of the outer batter sampled for perfect crispness, the rest torn off with abandon as you race to scarf up the lush yellow filling. Proper engagement with a *dosa* requires you to adopt a fingers-before-forks approach and give up any squeamishness about getting your hands messy; it might help to remember the old Indian saying that eating with cutlery is like making love through an interpreter.

Karnataka's dominant food culture is vegetarian, and the state's geographical and cultural diversity have created a wide variety of responses to the need to survive on rice and lentils: look out for *bisi-bele baath* (a rich and mildly spiced risotto-syle dish); and *puliyogare* (steamed rice soured with tamarind and seasoned with mustard seeds, curry leaves and fenugreek). Karnataka's other great staple is *ragi* (finger millet), most often served as *ragi mudde*, gooey brown dumplings that you tear apart and soak in *sambar* or *saaru* (a peppery lentil consommé similar to the Tamil *rasam*).

Mountainous Coorg has its own distinctive cuisine, headlined by the region's famous pork curry and the buttery steamed rice dumplings called *kadambuttu*. Along the Karnataka and Karavalli coasts, with their largely Syrian Christian and Muslim population, you'll find excellent fish and seafood dishes. Commonly found fish include *pearlspot* and *karimeen*, and these might be served simply fried, grilled or steamed, or in a *meen molee* (a potently spiced stew laden with coconut milk and tapioca).

Throughout India the best value food comes in the shape of the traditional *thali* (called *oota* in Karnataka), a complete feast often served on a banana leaf. A traditional *oota* begins with accompaniments – *kosambari* (a salad of pulses often mixed with cucumber), various hot spicy pickles and poppadums, after which comes a selection of spicy and sweet curries served with rice; then *saaru*, followed by rice and yoghurt. There's usually a bowl of sweet *payasam* (rice pudding) to finish off.

If you're unused to spicy food, go slow. Food is often spicier when you eat with families or at local places. Most restaurants are used to toning things down for foreign palates, so if you're worried about being overpowered, feel free to ask for the food to be made less spicy.

India has many delicious tropical **fruits**. Some are seasonal (eg mangoes, pineapples and jackfruit), while others (eg bananas, grapes and oranges) are available throughout the year. It is safe to eat the ones you can wash and peel.

Don't leave India without trying its superb range of indigenous **sweets**. A piece or two of milk-based *peda* or Mysore *pak* make a perfect sweet postscript to a cheap dinner.

Food hygiene

Food hygiene has improved immensely in recent years. However, you still need to take extra care, as flies abound and refrigeration in the hot weather may be inadequate and intermittent because of power cuts. It is safest to eat only freshly prepared food by ordering from the menu (especially meat and fish dishes). Be suspicious of salads and cut fruit, which may have been lying around for hours or washed in unpurified tap water – though salads served in top-end hotel restaurants and places primarily catering to foreigners can offer a blissful break from heavily spiced curries.

Drink

Drinking water used to be regarded as one of India's biggest hazards. It is still true that water from the tap or a well should never be considered safe to drink since public water supplies are often polluted. Bottled water is now widely available although not all bottled water is mineral water; most are simply purified water from an urban supply. Buy from a shop or stall, check the seal carefully (some companies now add a second clear plastic seal around the bottle top) and avoid street hawkers; when disposing bottles puncture the neck which prevents misuse but allows recycling.

Tea and **coffee** are safe and widely available. Both are normally served sweet, and with milk. If you wish, say 'no sugar' (*chini nahin*), 'no milk' (*dudh nahin*) when ordering. Alternatively, ask for a pot of tea and milk and sugar to be brought separately. Even in aspiring smart cafés, espresso or cappuccino may not turn out quite as you'd expect in the West.

Bottled **soft drinks** such as Coke, Pepsi, Teem, Limca, Thums Up and Gold Spot are universally available but always check the seal when you buy from a street stall. There are also several brands of fruit juice sold in cartons, including mango, pineapple and apple – Indian brands are very sweet. Don't add ice cubes as the water source may be contaminated. Take care with fresh fruit juices or *lassis* as ice is often added.

In the past **wines** and **spirits** were generally either imported and extremely expensive, or local and of poor quality. Now, the best Indian whisky, rum and brandy (IMFL or 'Indian Made Foreign Liquor') are widely accepted, as are good Champagnoise and other wines from Maharashtra. If you hanker after a bottle of imported wine, you will only find it in the top restaurants for at least Rs 800-1000.

For the urban elite, refreshing Indian **beers** are popular when eating out and are widely available. 'Pubs' have sprung up in the major cities. Elsewhere, seedy, all-male drinking dens in the larger cities are best avoided for women travellers, but can make quite an experience otherwise – you will sometimes be locked into cubicles for clandestine drinking. If that sounds unsavoury then head for the better hotel bars instead; prices aren't that steep.

In rural India, local rice, palm, cashew or date juice *toddy* and *arak* is deceptively potent.

Eating out

Choosing a good restaurant can be tricky if you're new to India. Many **local eateries** sport a grimy look that can be off-putting, yet serve brilliant and safe food, while swish five-star hotel restaurants that attract large numbers of tourists can dish up buffet food that leaves you crawling to the bathroom in the middle of the night. A large crowd of locals is always a good sign that the food is freshly cooked and good. Even fly-blown *dhabas* on the roadside can be safe, as long as you stick to freshly cooked meals and avoid timebombs such as deep-fried samosas that have been left in the sun for hours.

Many city restaurants and backpacker eateries offer a choice of so-called **European options** such as toasted sandwiches, stuffed pancakes, apple pies, fruit crumbles and cheesecakes. Italian favourites (pizzas, pastas) can be very different from what you are used to. Ice creams, on the other hand, can be exceptionally good; there are excellent Indian ones as well as some international brands.

Essentials A-Z

Accidents and emergencies

Contact the relevant emergency service (police T100, fire T101, ambulance T102) and your embassy. Make sure you obtain police/medical reports required for insurance claims.

Customs and duty free

Tourists are allowed to bring in all personal effects 'which may reasonably be required', without charge. The official customs allowance includes 200 cigarettes or 50 cigars, 0.95 litres of alcohol, a camera and a pair of binoculars. Valuable personal effects and professional equipment including jewellery, special camera equipment and lenses, laptop computers and sound and video recorders must in theory be declared on a Tourist Baggage Re-Export Form (TBRE) in order for them to be taken out of the country; in practice it's relatively unlikely that your bags will be inspected beyond a cursory x-ray. Nevertheless, it saves considerable frustration if you know the equipment serial numbers in advance and are ready to show them on the equipment. In addition to the forms, details of imported equipment may be entered into your passport. Save time by completing the formalities while waiting for your baggage. It is essential to keep these forms for showing to the customs when leaving India, otherwise considerable delays are very likely at the time of departure.

Prohibited items

The import of dangerous drugs, live plants, gold coins, gold and silver bullion and silver coins not in current use are either banned or subject to strict regulation. It is illegal to import firearms into India without special permission. Enquire at consular offices abroad for details.

Drugs

Certain areas, such as Gokarna and Hampi, have become associated with foreigners who take drugs. These are likely to attract local and foreign drug dealers but be aware that the government takes the misuse of drugs very seriously. Anyone charged with the illegal possession of drugs risks facing a fine of Rs 100,000 and a minimum 10 years' imprisonment. Several foreigners have been imprisoned for drugs-related offences in the last decade.

Electricity

India supply is 220-240 volts AC. Some top hotels have transformers. There may be pronounced variations in the voltage, and power cuts are common. Power back-up by generator or inverter is becoming more widespread, even in humble hotels, though it may not cover a/c. Socket sizes vary so take a universal adaptor; low-quality versions are available locally. Many hotels, even in the higher categories, don't have electric razor sockets. Invest in a stabilizer for a laptop.

Embassies and consulates

For information on visas and immigration, see page 137. For a comprehensive list of embassies (but not all consulates), see http://india.gov.in/overseas/indian_missions.php. Many embassies around the world are now outsourcing the visa process; this might affect how long it takes.

Festivals and public holidays

India has a wealth of festivals with many celebrated nationwide, while others are specific to a particular state or community or even a particular temple. Many fall on different dates each year depending on the Hindu lunar calendar; there's a thorough calendar of upcoming major and minor festivals at www.drikpanchang.com.

The Hindu calendar Hindus follow 2 distinct eras: the *Vikrama Samvat* which began in 57 BC and the *Salivahan Saka* which dates from AD 78 and has been the official Indian calendar since 1957. The *Saka* new year starts on 22 Mar and has the same length as the Gregorian calendar. The 29½-day lunar month with its 'dark' and 'bright' halves based on the new and full moons, are named after 12 constellations, and total a 354-day year. The calendar cleverly has an extra month (*adhik maas*) every 2½-3 years, to bring it in line with the solar year of 365 days coinciding with the Gregorian calendar of the West.

Some major national and regional festivals are listed below. A few count as national holidays including: **26 Jan**: **Republic Day**; **15 Aug**: **Independence Day**; **2 Oct**: **Mahatma Gandhi's Birthday**; and **25 Dec**: **Christmas Day**.

1 Jan New Year's Day is accepted officially when following the Gregorian calendar but there are regional variations that fall on different dates, often coinciding with spring/harvest time in Mar and Apr.

13-16 Jan The 4-day harvest festival of **Pongal** is celebrated with great fervour in areas with a large Tamil population. Doorsteps are decorated with *kolam* (geometric designs in coloured powder), cattle are worshipped, and vast pots of the eponymous rice dish are cooked. Elsewhere in the state, the day is celebrated as **Makar Sankranti**.

Jan-Mar This is **Kambala** season, with bullock races held each weekend in towns up and down the Karnataka coast, especially around Mangalore and Udupi.

Feb Vasant Panchami, the spring festival, when people wear bright yellow clothes to mark the advent of the season, is celebrated with singing, dancing and feasting.

Feb-Mar Maha Sivaratri marks the night when Siva danced his celestial dance of destruction (*Tandava*), which is celebrated with feasting and fairs at Siva temples, but preceded by a night of devotional readings and hymn singing.

Apr/May Buddha Jayanti, the 1st full moon night in Apr/May marks the birth of the Buddha.

15 Aug Independence Day, a national secular holiday, is marked by special events. **Vinayaka Chaturthi,** known elsewhere in India as **Ganesh Chaturthi**, is the day when the elephant-headed god of good omen is shown special reverence. On the last of the 5-day festival after harvest, clay images of Ganesh are taken in procession with dancers and musicians, and are immersed in the sea, river or pond.

Aug/Sep Janmashtami, the birth of Krishna is celebrated at midnight at Krishna temples.

Sep/Oct The festival of **Navaratri** has many local variations throughout India. It is celebrated as Dasara in Mysore, where the goddess Chamundeshwari is honoured for killing the demon Mahishasura (after whom the city is named). The lights on the palace stay illuminated for all 10 nights, and the idol of Chamundeshwari comes down from her hilltop temple to parade through the city on the back of a decorated elephant.

2 Oct Gandhi Jayanti, Mahatma Gandhi's birthday, is remembered with prayer meetings and devotional singing.

Oct/Nov Diwali/Deepavali (*Sanskrit ideepa* lamp), the festival of lights, is celebrated in Karnataka. Some Hindus celebrate Krishna's victory over the demon Narakasura, some Rama's return after his 14 years' exile in the forest when citizens lit his way with oil lamps. The festival falls on the dark *chaturdasi* (14th) night (the one preceding the new moon), when rows of lamps or candles are lit in remembrance, and *rangolis* are painted on the floor as a sign of welcome. Fireworks have become an integral part of the celebration which are often set off days before Diwali. Equally, Lakshmi, the Goddess of Wealth (as well as Ganesh) is worshipped by merchants and the business community who open the new financial year's account on the day. Most people wear new clothes; some play games of chance.

1 Nov Karnataka Rajyothsava. The anniversary of the state's foundation is a public holiday, marked by red and yellow flags flying from every rickshaw and restaurant counter.

25 Dec Christmas Day sees Indian Christians celebrate the birth of Christ in much the same way as in the West; many churches hold services/Mass at midnight. There is an air of festivity in city markets which are specially decorated and illuminated.

31 Dec Over **New Year's Eve** hotel prices peak and large supplements are added for meals and entertainment in the upper category hotels. Some churches mark the night with a Midnight Mass.

Muslim holy days These are fixed according to the lunar calendar. According to the Gregorian calendar, they tend to fall 11 days earlier each year, dependent on the sighting of the new moon.

Ramadan is the start of the month of fasting when all Muslims (except young children, the very elderly, the sick, pregnant women and travellers) must abstain from food and drink, from sunrise to sunset. Ramadan is most widely observed in the Malabar region of northern Karnataka; during this time many restaurants remain closed until sundown.

Id ul Fitr is the 3-day festival that marks the end of Ramadan.

Id-ul-Zuha/Bakr-Id is when Muslims commemorate Ibrahim's sacrifice of his son according to God's commandment; the main time of pilgrimage to Mecca (the Hajj). It is marked by the sacrifice of a goat, feasting and alms giving.

Muharram is when the killing of the Prophet's grandson, Hussain, is commemorated by Shi'a Muslims. Decorated *tazias* (replicas of the martyr's tomb) are carried in procession by devout wailing followers who beat their chests to express their grief. Shi'as fast for the 10 days.

Health

Local populations in India are exposed to a range of health risks not encountered in the Western world. Many of the diseases are major problems for the local poor and destitute and, although the risk to travellers is more remote, they cannot be ignored. Obviously 5-star travel is going to carry less risk than backpacking on a budget.

Health care in the region is varied. There are many excellent private and government clinics/hospitals. As with all medical care, first impressions count. It's worth contacting your embassy or consulate on arrival and asking where the recommended (ie those used by diplomats) clinics are. You can also ask about locally recommended medical do's and don'ts. If you do get ill, and you have the opportunity, you should also ask your medical insurer whether they are satisfied that the medical centre/hospital you have been referred to is of a suitable standard.

Before you go

Ideally, you should see your GP or travel clinic at least 6 weeks before your departure for general advice on travel risks, malaria and vaccinations. Make sure you have travel insurance, get a dental check (especially if you are going to be away for more than a month), know your own blood group and if you suffer a long-term condition such as diabetes or epilepsy make sure someone knows or that you have a Medic Alert bracelet/necklace with this information on it. Remember that it is risky to buy medicinal tablets abroad because the doses may differ and India has a huge trade in false drugs.

Vaccinations

If you need vaccinations, see your doctor well in advance of your travel. Most courses must be completed by a minimum of 4 weeks. Travel clinics may provide rapid courses of vaccination, but are likely to be more expensive. The following vaccinations are recommended: typhoid, polio, tetanus, infectious hepatitis and diptheria. For details of malaria prevention, contact your GP or local travel clinic.

The following vaccinations may also be considered: rabies, possibly BCG (since TB is still common in the region) and in some cases meningitis (if you're staying in the country for a long time). Yellow fever is not required in India but you may be asked to show a certificate if you have travelled from Africa or South America. Japanese encephalitis may be required for rural travel at certain times of the year (mainly rainy seasons). An effective oral cholera vaccine (Dukoral) is now available as 2 doses providing 3 months' protection.

Websites

British Travel Health Association (UK), www.btha.org The official website of an organization of travel health professionals.

Fit for Travel, www.fitfortravel.scot. nhs.uk This site from Scotland provides a quick A-Z of vaccine and travel health advice requirements for each country.

Foreign and Commonwealth Office (FCO) (UK), www.fco.gov.uk A key travel advice site, with useful information on the country, people, climate and lists the UK embassies/consulates. The site also promotes the concept of 'know before you go' and encourages travel insurance and appropriate travel health advice. It has links to Department of Health travel advice site.

The Health Protection Agency, www.hpa.org.uk Up-to-date malaria advice guidelines for travel around the world. It gives specific advice about the right drugs for each location. It also has useful information for those who are pregnant, suffering from epilepsy or planning to travel with children.

Medic Alert (UK), www.medicalalert. com This is the website of the foundation that produces bracelets and necklaces for those with existing medical problems. Once you have ordered your bracelet/necklace you write your key medical details on paper inside it, so that if you collapse, a medic can identify you as having epilepsy or a nut allergy, etc.

Travel Screening Services (UK), www.travelscreening.co.uk A private clinic dedicated to integrated travel health. The clinic gives vaccine, travel health advice, email and SMS text vaccine reminders and screens returned travellers for tropical diseases.

World Health Organisation, www. who.int The WHO site has links to the *WHO Blue Book* on travel advice. This lists the diseases in different regions of the world. It describes vaccination schedules and makes clear which countries have yellow fever vaccination certificate requirements and malarial risk.

Books

International Travel and Health World Health Organisation Geneva, ISBN 92-4-15802-6-7.

Lankester, T, *The Travellers Good Health Guide*, ISBN 0-85969-827-0.

Warrell, D and Anderson, A (eds), *Expedition Medicine (The Royal Geographic Society)*, ISBN 1-86197-040-4.

Young Pelton, R, Aral, C and Dulles, W, *The World's Most Dangerous Places*, ISBN 1-566952-140-9.

Language

→ *See page 139 for useful words and phrases.*

The state language of Karnataka is Kannada, a member of the Dravidian family of South Indian languages. Except in Bengaluru, Hindi – the official national language – is little known, and given the difficulty of learning Kannada, English acts as the lingua franca between locals and visitors. It is widely spoken in towns and cities and even in quite remote villages it is usually not difficult to find someone who speaks at least a little English. Outside of major tourist sites, other European languages are almost completely unknown. The accent in which English is spoken is often affected strongly by the mother tongue of the speaker and there have been changes in common grammar which can make it sound unusual. Many of these changes have become standard Indian English usage, as valid as any other varieties of English used around the world.

Money

Indian currency is the Indian Rupee (Re/Rs). It is not possible to purchase these before you arrive. If you want cash on arrival it is best to get it at the airport bank, although see if an ATM is available as airport rates are not very generous. Rupee notes are printed in denominations of Rs 1000, 500, 100, 50, 20, 10. The rupee is divided into 100 paise. Coins are minted in denominations of Rs 5, Rs 2, Rs 1 and 50 paise. **Note** Carry money in a money belt worn under clothing. Have a small amount in an easily accessible place.

Exchange rates *(Feb 2015)*
UK £1 = Rs 96, €1 = Rs 70, US$1 = Rs 62.

Credit cards

Major credit cards are increasingly acceptable in the main centres, though in smaller cities and towns it is still rare to be able to pay by credit card. Payment by credit card can sometimes be more expensive than payment by cash, whilst some credit card companies charge a premium on cash withdrawals. **Visa** and **MasterCard** have a growing number of ATMs in major cities and several banks offer withdrawal facilities for Cirrus and Maestro cardholders. It is however easy to obtain a cash advance against a credit card. Railway reservation centres in major cities take payment for train tickets by Visa card which can be very quick as the queue is short, although they cannot be used for Tourist Quota tickets.

Currency cards

If you don't want to carry lots of cash, pre-paid currency cards allow you to preload money from your bank account, fixed at the day's exchange rate. They look like a credit or debit card and are issued by specialist money changing companies, such as **Travelex** and **Caxton FX**, as well as the **Post Office**. You can top up and check your balance by phone, online and sometimes by text.

Traveller's cheques (TCs)

TCs issued by reputable companies (eg **Thomas Cook**, **American Express**) are widely accepted. They can be easily exchanged at small local travel agents and tourist internet cafés but are rarely used directly for payment. Try to avoid changing at banks, where the process can be time consuming; opt for hotels and agents instead, take large denomination cheques and change enough to last for some days.

ATMs

By far the most convenient method of accessing money, ATMs are all over India, usually attended by security guards, with most banks offering some services to holders of overseas cards. Banks whose ATMs will issue cash against Cirrus and Maestro cards, as well as Visa and MasterCard, include **Bank of Baroda**, **Citibank**, **HDFC**, **HSBC**, **ICICI**, **IDBI**, **Punjab National Bank**, **State Bank of India (SBI)**, **Standard Chartered** and **UTI**. A withdrawal fee is usually charged by the issuing bank on top of the conversion charges applied by your own bank. Fraud prevention measures quite often result in travellers having their cards blocked by the bank when unexpected overseas transactions occur; advise your bank of your travel plans before leaving.

Changing money

The **State Bank of India** and several others in major towns are authorized to deal in foreign exchange. Some give cash against Visa/MasterCard (eg **ANZ**, **Bank of Baroda,** who print a list of their participating branches, and **Andhra Bank**). The larger cities have licensed money changers with offices usually in the commercial sector. Changing money through unauthorized dealers is illegal. Premiums on the currency black market are very small and highly risky. Large hotels change money 24 hrs a day for guests, but banks often give a substantially better rate of exchange. It is best to exchange money on arrival at the airport bank or the Thomas Cook counter. Many international flights arrive during the night and it is generally far easier and less time consuming to change money at the airport than in the city. You should be given a foreign currency encashment certificate when you change money through a bank or authorized dealer; ask for one if it is not automatically given. It allows you to change Indian rupees back to your own currency on departure. It also enables you to use rupees to pay hotel bills or buy air tickets for which payment in foreign exchange may be required. The certificates are only valid for 3 months.

Cost of travelling

Most food, accommodation and public transport, especially rail and bus, is exceptionally cheap, although inflation is pushing prices up at a drastic rate and the cost of basic food items such as rice, lentils, tomatoes and onions have skyrocketed. There is a widening range of moderately priced but clean hotels and restaurants outside the big cities, making it possible to get a great deal for your money. Budget travellers sharing a room, taking public transport, avoiding souvenir stalls, and eating nothing but rice and dhal can get away with a budget of Rs 600-900 (about US$10-15 or £6-10) a day. This sum leaps up if you drink alcohol (still cheap by European standards at about US$2, £1 or Rs 80 for a pint), smoke foreign-brand cigarettes or want to have your own wheels (you can expect to spend between Rs 150 and Rs 300 to hire a Honda per day). Those planning to stay in fairly comfortable hotels and use taxis sightseeing should budget at US$50-80 (£30-50) a day. Then again you could always check into **Orange County** in Coorg for Christmas and notch up an impressive US$600 (£350) bill on your B&B alone. India can be a great place to pick and choose, save a little on basic accommodation and then treat yourself to the type of meal you could only dream of affording back home. Also, be prepared to spend a fair amount more in Bengaluru, where the cost of living is higher and where it's worth. In general, a newspaper costs Rs 5 and breakfast for 2 with coffee can come to as little as Rs 50 in a South Indian 'hotel', but if you intend to eat banana pancakes or pasta by the beach in Gokarna, you can expect to pay more like Rs 50-150 a plate.

Opening hours

Banks are open Mon-Fri 1030-1430, Sat 1030-1230. Top hotels sometimes have a 24-hr money changing service. **Government offices** open Mon-Fri 0930-1700, Sat 0930-1300 (some open on alternate Sat only). **Post offices** open Mon-Fri 1000-1700, often shutting for lunch, and Sat mornings. **Shops** open Mon-Sat 0930-1800. Bazars keep longer hours.

Safety

Personal security

In general the threats to personal security for travellers in India are remarkably small. However, incidents of petty theft and violence directed specifically at tourists have been on the increase so care is necessary in some places, and basic common sense needs to be used with respect to looking after valuables. Follow the same precautions you would when at home. There have been incidents of sexual assault in and around the main tourist beach centres, particularly after full moon parties in South India. Avoid wandering alone outdoors late at night in these places. During daylight hours be careful in remote places, especially when alone.

If you are under threat, scream loudly. Be very cautious before accepting food or drink from casual acquaintances, as it may be drugged – though note that Indians on a long train journey will invariably try to share their snacks with you, and balance caution with the opportunity to interact.

A string of notorious sexual assaults in North India in recent years have raised concerns for female travellers, especially those travelling solo. Whilst these have not been directed at Western women – and whilst mild-mannered Karnataka is certainly not New Delhi – you may in some places experience verbal (and occasionally physical) harassment – an unfortunate result of the sexual repression latent in Indian culture, combined with a young male population whose only access to sex education is via dingy cybercafés. Unaccompanied women are most vulnerable in major cities, crowded bazars, beach resorts and tourist centres where men may follow them and attempt to touch them. Festival nights are particularly bad for this, but it is always best to be accompanied at night, especially when travelling by rickshaw or taxi in towns.

The most important measure to ensure respect is to dress appropriately, in loose-fitting, non-see-through clothes, covering shoulders, arms and legs (such as a *salwaar kameez*, which can be made to fit in around 24 hrs for around Rs 400-800). Take advantage, too, of the gender segregation on public transport, to avoid hassle and to talk to local women.

The best response to staring, whether lascivious or simply curious, is to avert your eyes down and away. This is not the submissive gesture it might seem, but an effective tool to communicate that you have no interest in any further interaction. Aggressively staring back or confronting the starer can be construed as a come-on.

If you are harassed, it can be effective to make a scene. Be firm and clear if you don't wish to speak to someone, and be prepared to raise an alarm if anything unpleasant threatens.

Travel advice
It is better to seek advice from your consulate than from travel agencies. Before you travel you can contact: **British Foreign & Commonwealth Office Travel Advice Unit**, T0845-850 2829, www.fco.gov.uk; **US State Department's Bureau of Consular Affairs**, Overseas Citizens Services, Room 4800, Department of State, Washington, DC 20520-4818, USA, T202-647 1488, http://travel.state.gov; or **Australian Department of Foreign Affairs Canberra**, Australia, T02-6261 3305, www.smarttraveller.gov.au. Canadian official advice is on **www.voyage.gc.ca**.

Theft
Theft is not uncommon. It is best to keep TCs, passports and valuables with you at all times. Don't regard hotel rooms as being automatically safe; even hotel safes don't guarantee secure storage. Avoid leaving valuables near open windows even when you are in the room. Use your own padlock in a budget hotel when you go out. Pickpockets and other thieves operate in the big cities. Crowded areas are particularly high risk. Take special care of your belongings when getting on or off public transport.

If you have items stolen, they should be reported to the police as soon as possible. Keep a separate record of vital documents, including passport details and numbers of TCs. Larger hotels will be able to assist in contacting and dealing with the police. The paperwork involved in reporting losses can be time consuming and irritating and your own documentation (eg passport and visas) may be demanded.

In some states the police occasionally demand bribes, though you should not assume that if procedures move slowly you are automatically being expected to offer a bribe. The traffic police are tightening up on traffic offences in some places. They have the right to make on-the-spot fines for speeding and illegal parking. If you face a fine, insist on a receipt. If you have to go to a police station, try to take someone with you.

If you face really serious problems (eg in connection with a driving accident), contact your consular office as quickly as possible. You should ensure you always have your international driving licence and motorbike or car documentation with you.

Confidence tricksters are particularly common where people are on the move, notably around railway stations or places where budget tourists gather. A common plea is some sudden and desperate calamity; sometimes a letter will be produced in English to back up the claim. The demands are likely to increase sharply if sympathy is shown.

Telephone

The international code for India is +91. International Direct Dialling is widely available in privately run call booths, usually labelled on yellow boards with the letters 'PCO-STD-ISD'. You dial the call yourself, and the time and cost are displayed on a computer screen. Cheap rate (2100-0600) means long queues may form outside booths.

Telephone calls from hotels are usually more expensive (check the price before calling), though some will allow local calls free of charge. Internet phone booths, usually associated with cybercafés, are the cheapest way of calling overseas.

A double ring repeated regularly means it is ringing; equal tones with equal pauses means engaged (similar to the UK). If calling a mobile, rather than ringing, you might hear music while you wait for an answer.

One disadvantage of the tremendous pace of the telecommunications revolution is the fact that millions of telephone numbers go out of date every year. Current telephone directories themselves are often out of date and some of the numbers given in this book will have been changed even as we go to press. **Directory enquiries**, T197, can be helpful but works only for the local area code.

Mobile phones are for sale everywhere, as are local SIM cards that allow you to make calls within India and overseas at much lower rates than using a 'roaming' service from your normal provider at home – sometimes for as little as Rs 0.5 per min. Arguably the best service is provided by the government carrier **BSNL/MTNL** but security provisions make connecting to the service virtually impossible for foreigners. Private companies such as **Airtel**, **Vodafone**, **Reliance** and **Tata Indicom** are easier to sign up with, but the deals they offer can be befuddling and are frequently changed. To connect you'll need to complete a form, have a local address or receipt showing the address of your hotel, and present photocopies of your passport and visa plus 2 passport photos to an authorized re-seller – most phone dealers will be able to help, and can also sell top-up. **Univercell**, www.univercell.in, and **The Mobile Store**, www.themobilestore.in, are 2 widespread and efficient chains selling phones and SIM cards.

India is divided into a number of 'calling circles' or regions, and if you travel outside the region where your connection is based you will pay higher charges for making and receiving calls, and any problems that may occur – with 'unverified' documents, for example – can be much harder to resolve.

Time

India doesn't change its clocks, so from the last Sun in Oct to the last Sun in Mar the time is GMT +5½ hrs, and the rest of the year it's +4½ hrs (USA, EST +10½ and +9½ hrs; Australia, EST -5½ and -4½ hrs).

Tipping

A tip of Rs 10 to a bellboy carrying luggage in a modest hotel (Rs 20 in a higher category) would be appropriate. In upmarket restaurants, a 10% tip is acceptable when service is not already included, while in places serving very cheap meals, round off the bill with small change. Indians don't normally tip taxi drivers but a small extra is welcomed. Porters at airports and railway stations often have a fixed rate displayed but will usually press for more. Ask fellow passengers what a fair rate is.

Tourist information

There are **Government of India** tourist offices in the state capitals, as well as state tourist offices (sometimes **Tourism Development Corporations**) in the major cities and a few important sites. They produce their own tourist literature, either free or sold at a nominal price, and some also have lists of city hotels and paying guest options. The quality of material is improving though maps are often poor. Many offer tours of the city, neighbouring sights and overnight and regional packages. Some run modest hotels and midway motels with restaurants and may also arrange car hire and guides. The staff in the regional and local offices are usually helpful.

Visas and immigration

For embassies and consulates, see page 129. Virtually all foreign nationals, including children, require a visa to enter India. Nationals of Bhutan and Nepal only require a suitable means of identification. The rules regarding visas change frequently and arrangements for application and collection also vary from town to town so it is essential to check details and costs with the relevant embassy or consulate. These remain closed on Indian national holidays. Many consulates and embassies are currently outsourcing the visa process; check the website of **VFS Global,** www.vfsglobal.co.uk, in your country for the current rules and application times. Note that visas are valid from the date granted, not from the date of entry.

Recently the Indian government has introduced visas on arrival for residents of almost all countries, providing you are only travelling for tourism purposes. (Pakistan, Sudan, Afghanistan, Iran, Iraq, Nigeria, Sri Lanka and Somalia are the exceptions). The **Tourist visa on arrival (TVOA)** is valid for stays of up to 30 days. However, this does not mean you can just jump on a plane this afternoon and waltz into India in time for breakfast. You still need to apply in advance at **https://indianvisaonline.gov.in/visa/tvoa.html**, at least 4 days but no more than 30 days before your arrival in India, and pay a fee of US$60. However, for short visits it saves the hassle of posting or collecting your passport, and as such is a sign of improvement. You can apply for a maximum of 2 TVOAs per year.

For longer stays, or if you're travelling to Bengaluru for work or business, the process of getting a visa has actually become harder. The Indian government now intends to collect biometric data (fingerprints and facial images) from all foreign visitors. In theory, this means that instead of posting your application and receiving it in the post, you have to make an appointment and turn up in person at your nearest application centre. However, attempts to introduce data collection in Australia have been 'indefinitely deferred' as of Jan 2015 – possibly a shape of things to come elsewhere.

Anyone staying in India for a period of more than 180 days (6 months) must register at a convenient **Foreigners' Registration Office**. They will also need to get an income tax clearance exemption certificate from the Foreign Section of the Income Tax Department in Delhi, Mumbai, Kolkata or Chennai.

Tourist For most purposes you'll require a straightforward Tourist Visa. This is typically valid for 3-6 months, though citizens of some countries may be granted a 5-year visa on request. Multiple entries permitted. Rules introduced in 2010 that required visitors leaving for Nepal or Sri Lanka to remain outside India for a minimum of 2 months have since been scrapped.

Business 3-6 months or up to 2 years with multiple entry. A letter from the company giving the nature of business is required.

5 year For those of Indian origin only, who have held Indian passports.

Student Valid up to 1 year from the date of issue. Attach a letter of acceptance from Indian institution and an AIDS test certificate. Allow up to 3 months for approval.

Visa extensions Applications should be made to the Foreigners' Regional Registration Offices at New Delhi, Mumbai, Kolkata or Chennai, or an office of the Superintendent of Police in the District Headquarters. After 6 months, you must leave India and apply for a new visa – the Nepal office is known to be difficult.

Weights and measures

Metric is in universal use in the cities. In remote areas local measures are sometimes used. One lakh is 100,000 and 1 crore is 10 million.

Useful words & phrases

Basics

hello, good morning, goodbye	Namaskara/ hogi baruttene	yes	Houdu
thank you	Dhanyavaadagalu	no	Illa
no, thank you	Illa, dhanyavaada	never mind/ that's all right	parvagilla
excuse me, sorry	Kshamisi		

Questions

What is your name?	Nimma hesar yenu?	Not very well	Mai ushyar illa
My name is ...	Nan hesaru ...	Where is the ...?	Id yellide ...?
Pardon?	Kshamisi?	Who is?	Yaaru?
How are you?	Neevu hegidira?	What is this?	Yean idu?
I am well, thanks, and you?	Naanu chennagidini. Dhanyavaada. Neevu?		

Shopping

How much?	Yeshtu?	That is very expensive	Idu thumba jaasti
That makes (20) rupees	Idu ippat rupai	Make it a bit cheaper	Swalpa kadimay maadi

The hotel

What is the room charge?	Room charge yeshtu?	Is there a large room?	Yavadu dodda room idiya?
Please show the room	Dayavittu room thorisi	Please clean it	Davavuttu idanna clean maadi
Is there an air-conditioned room?	Yavadu air-conditioned room idiya?	Are there clean sheets/blanket?	Illi clean bedsheetu mattu blanket idiya?
Is there hot water?	Bisi neer idiya?	Bill please	Bill kodi
... a bathroom/fan/ mosquito net	... ond bathroomu/ fanu/solle nettu		

Travel

Where's the railway station?	*Railway station yellide?*	Go straight on	*Seeda hogi*
		Nearby	*Pakkada*
How much is the ticket to Hassan?	*Hassan hogakke ticket kharch yeshtu?*	Please wait here	*Dayavittu ill wait maadi*
When does the Hassan bus leave?	*Hassangay bus yavaga hogatte?*	Please come at 8	*Davayavittu ent ghante gay banni*
		Quickly	*Jaldi*
How much?	*Yeshtu?*	Stop	*Iri*
Left/right	*Leftu/rightu*		

Time and days

right now	*ivaaga*	day	*dina*
month	*tingalu*	week	*vaara*
morning	*beliggay*		
year	*varsha*	Sunday	*bhaanuvaara*
afternoon	*madhyana*	Monday	*somavaara*
evening	*saayankaala*	Tuesday	*mangalvaara*
night	*raatri*	Wednesday	*bhuduvaara*
today	*ivattu*	Thursday	*guruvaara*
tomorrow	*naale*	Friday	*shukarvaara*
yesterday	*nenne*	Saturday	*shanivaara*

Numbers

one	*ondu*	fourteen	*hadinaalakku*
two	*yeradu*	fifteen	*hadinaidu*
three	*mooru*	sixteen	*hadinaaru*
four	*naalakku*	seventeen	*hadinolu*
five	*aidu*	eighteen	*hadinentu*
six	*aaru*	nineteen	*hatthombatthu*
seven	*yeloo*	twenty	*ippathu*
eight	*yentu*	hundred	*nooru*
nine	*ombatthu*	two hundred	*innooru*
ten	*hatthu*	one thousand	*ond saavra*
eleven	*hannondu*	two thousand	*yerad saavra*
twelve	*hanneradu*	hundred thousand	*ond laksha*
thirteen	*hadimooru*		

Basic vocabulary

big	*dodda*	which	*yaavadu?*
small	*chikka*	who	*yaaru?*
café/food stall	*oota stall*	why	*yaake?*
chemist	*medical angadi*		
clean	*cleanu*	Please show the menu	*Dayavittu menu thorisi*
closed	*mucchalaagide*	No chillies please	*Dayavittu masale haakbedi*
cold	*sheeta*		
day	*dina*	sugar/milk/ice	*sakkare/haalu/ice*
dirty	*kolaku*	A bottle of water please	*Ond bottle neer kodi*
English	*Englis*		
excellent	*atiuttama*	sweet/savoury	*sihi/khara*
food/to eat	*oota/tinnakke*	spoon	*chamache*
hot (spicy)	*bisi (masale)*	fork	*mullu chamache*
hot (temp)	*bisilu*	knife	*chaaku*
luggage	*laggageu*	chicken	*koli*
medicine	*oushadi*	fish	*meenu*
newspaper	*samachaarapatrike*	meat	*maamsa*
of course, sure	*khanditavaagi*	prawns	*sigaadigalu*
open	*tere*	vegetables	*tharakaari*
police station	*police thaane*	aubergine	*nelagulla*
road	*raste*	cabbage	*ele kosu*
room	*room*	carrots	*gajjari*
shop	*angadi*	cauliflower	*hoo kosu*
sick (ill)	*mai ushyar illa*	mushroom	*anabe*
silk	*reshami*	onion	*iruli*
that	*adu*	okra, ladies' fingers	*bende kaayi*
this	*idu*	peas	*bataani*
town	*ooru*	potato	*aloo gadde*
water	*neeru*	spinach	*paalaka*
what	*yenu?*	plain boiled rice	*sarala beyisida anna*
when	*yaavaga?*		
where	*yelli?*		

Index → *Entries in bold refer to maps*

FOOTPRINT

Features

Credits

Footprint credits

Editor: Nicola Gibbs
Production and layout: Emma Bryers
Maps: Kevin Feeney
Colour section: Angus Dawson

Publisher: Patrick Dawson
Managing Editor: Felicity Laughton
Administration: Elizabeth Taylor
Advertising sales and marketing:
John Sadler, Kirsty Holmes

Photography credits

Front cover: Mysore Palace
Copyright: Grzegorz Kielbasa/
Dreamstime.com
Back cover top: Hampi
Copyright: Skouatroulio/Dreamstime.com
Back cover bottom: Jog waterfalls
Copyright: Mnsanthoshkumar/
Dreamstime.com

Colour section
Inside front cover: shutterstock:
f9photos; superstock: Luis Davilla/age
fotostock, Tips Images/Tips Images.
Page 1: dreamstime: Katoosha/
Dreamstime.com. **Page 2:** shutterstock:
Pikoso.kz. **Page 4:** shutterstock: Claudine
Van Massenhove; superstock: Hemis.
fr/Hemis.fr. **Page 5:** dreamstime:
Andrew Allport/Dreamstime.com,
Nina Moskovchenko/Dreamstime.
com; superstock: Martin Siepmann/
Westend61, Olaf Krüger/imagebrok/
imageBROKER. **Page 6:** shutterstock: Waj;
superstock: Cyrille Gibot/age fotostock,
Hemis.fr/Hemis.fr, Tibor Bognár/age
fotostock. **Page 8:** superstock: Eye
Ubiquitous/Eye Ubiquitous.

Printed in Spain by GraphyCems

Publishing information

Footprint Bangalore & Karnataka
2nd edition
© Footprint Handbooks Ltd
April 2015

ISBN: 978 1 909268 63 0
CIP DATA: A catalogue record for this
book is available from the British Library

® Footprint Handbooks and the
Footprint mark are a registered
trademark of Footprint Handbooks Ltd

Published by Footprint
6 Riverside Court
Lower Bristol Road
Bath BA2 3DZ, UK
T +44 (0)1225 469141
footprinttravelguides.com

Distributed in the USA by
National Book Network, Inc.

Every effort has been made to ensure
that the facts in this guidebook are
accurate. However, travellers should still
obtain advice from consulates, airlines,
etc about travel and visa requirements
before travelling. The authors and
publishers cannot accept responsibility
for any loss, injury or inconvenience
however caused.